Candle Making

PELHAM CRAFT BOOKS

Candle Making

Terence McLaughlin

DRAKE PUBLISHERS INC
New York

ISBN 0-87749-561-0

Library of Congress Catalog Card Number 73-10903

Published in 1974 by
Drake Publishers Inc
381 Park Avenue South
New York, N. Y. 10016

Printed in Great Britain

Contents

Illustrations

Most of these candles are reproduced by permission of The Candles Shop, 89 Parkway, London NW1. The fireman's helmet in Plate 6 is by P. S. Bennett.

Introduction

Mankind has loved the friendly light of candles for almost as long as men have used fire. Even the cave-men lighted their simple homes with reeds or pine branches soaked in the fat of animals they had killed, and the caves at Lascaux still bear the sooty marks where the prehistoric cave-painters put their smoky torches to illuminate their ageless record of the time – pictures of long-lost animals like the gigantic aurochs, wolves, and tigers.

Wherever early men hunted for honey, they also found beeswax, and the warm light of the beeswax candle has been associated with civilisation ever since the early Egyptians, around 3200 B.C., left beeswax candles in the tombs of their great men and women to light their way to the Field of Rushes and the Field of Offerings – this was over a thousand years before similar beeswax lights were left for the young king Tutankhamun.

In Crete, in the Minoan civilisation of about 3000 B.C., which has left so many records of its life in the legends of the Greeks, candles were made of beeswax, usually in a cone shape round a reed for a wick, and used extensively to light the palace of King Minos. One can imagine the Minoan accountants poring over their stocktaking by the light of a beeswax cone. The accounts, written in that mysterious language called Linear B, are still with us.

All around the Middle East in early times, candles were made either from beeswax, or from tallow rendered down from animal fat, mostly that of cattle and sheep. The light of a candle was regarded as a comfort, protection, and also as a symbol of peace and understanding.

'I shall light a candle of understanding in thine heart, which shall not be put out,' said Esdras, and one of the most potent symbols of the fall of Babylon was the fact that 'the light of a candle shall shine no more.' Candles have been symbols of understanding and worship at many altars as well as Christian ones, and many of the most beautiful examples of the craft of candle making have been perfected for religious use. Roman Catholic altar candles have always traditionally been made of beeswax, and this wax, with its pleasant smell of honey and its soft light was used extensively for churches and for the very richest homes and courts.

By medieval times, candle making was divided between the Wax Chandlers, who made the superior wax candles by rolling beeswax into cylinders, and the Tallow Chandlers who worked with the inferior, but far more common, animal fats. In the thirteenth century and for many years afterwards the tallow chandlers would travel from large house to large house, bringing their own tallow or using the fat saved by thrifty housekeepers, and make tallow dips: these were reeds or lengths of flax dipped into the melted tallow until they had a sufficient coating of the fat to give a good light when burning. They also gave much smell and smoke, but the houses of those days were no strangers to smell and smoke, with their open fireplaces and primitive cooking methods.

These dips, rushlights, and candles were essential to the normal life of larger houses, and servants who worked for the king and his richer nobles would expect an allowance of candles as part of their wages. The allowance was jealously graded according to the rank and importance of the official, and the number of candles allotted to a steward or butler was watched as carefully and enviously by his fellow-servants as the size of the modern company executive's desk or carpet among his colleagues.

By the nineteenth century, candles were improving as new waxes were introduced, but their life as a useful means of illumination was already on the wane, for first gas and then electricity came along to replace them.

But despite all the modern methods, candles live on, and the craft of making decorative candles has never been more popular. What is so fascinating about a candle, and the magic of candle-light?

First there is the constant change and movement as the flame alters its shape and size in every slight current of air. A flame seems alive: compared with the uniform glare of the electric bulb it moves and undulates like a tiny bright dancer tracing out a complex pattern in light. The wax itself glows inside as the flame moves, and the colours of the candle, if it is a decorated one, show up as mysterious moving patterns.

If you want to give a romantic dinner party, you light your table with candles, not a 500-watt spotlight. The candle-light encourages conversation, it makes a centre for people to concentrate their gaze, and it provides a host of flickering shadows for the guests to hide themselves in if they want to talk seriously.

Candles are easy to make, and the materials are not expensive or difficult to obtain; very often they can be used again if your first attempts don't come out quite right. No very special equipment is needed, and you can choose from a vast range of styles, from the simplest dips to the most elaborate sculptural projects.

One further point. I believe that candles are made to burn, and all the candles described in this book are 'practical' ones that will give a good light as well as looking attractive. When you start making candles, you may find that the results look so fine that you cannot bear to put a match to them, but at least try some of them actually alight. For one thing, if the candle 'bug' gets hold of you, you will have so many candles around that you can afford to burn some of them. But the best reason for trying out your candles by actually burning them, is that the glow of the flame can make a fairly ordinary-looking candle into something really charming. Just as good lighting enhances the appearance of a picture on the wall, or a piece of sculpture, so does the light of the candle flame transform the colours and modelling of candles.

Wax is slightly transparent, so the light from the flame goes not only outwards but downwards into the body of the candle. You will often be surprised how differ-ent the colours and textures of your candles look when they are alight – the flat colours of the dyed wax take on an internal glow, and details that look quite dull on the unlighted candle may cast odd and interesting shadows from the candle flame.

Chapter 1

Materials

In the days when the tallow chandlers made their rounds, turning out candles for every large household, there were only two materials available for the task – beeswax and tallow. Beeswax was in short supply and expensive, so it was only practicable for the very richest household, and for church candles, so most people had to make do with tallow. This fat was melted down from left-over beef and mutton by the butchers, and sold to the tallow chandlers, but most thrifty housekeepers saved the fats from their own cooking operations and used this for making soap and candles. 'Household stuff' as it was called, was an important ingredient in a good many home manufactures.

It is easy to imagine the sort of candles that were made in this way. Even refined tallow has a very unpleasant smell when it is hot, and when it actually burns it produces that peculiarly penetrating, eye-watering effect that is familiar from accidents with overheated fat – the actual material is called *acrolein* from its acrid smell. For this reason everyone except the tallow chandlers must have been heartily glad when better materials became available. Of course, if you want to make tallow candles as a piece of historical research, by all means do so, but don't be tempted to light them in a crowded room to show them off to your friends!

WAXES
Paraffin wax
Paraffin wax is the most important of all the waxes used in candle making. It comes as a hard, smooth material that is usually completely white, although some grades have a slightly cream colour. It has a polished appearance and is slightly transparent – *translucent* is the better word. This translucency produces many of the charms of paraffin wax as a material for decorative candle making, as many attractive effects can be achieved by displaying light or colour through a thin layer of white or coloured wax. For example, many candles are made in such a way that the flame burns down in a hollow in a block of wax, and the light shines through the surrounding wax like a distant lantern. 'Balloon candles' (see Chapter 5) are made with decorative colour patterns inside a thin layer of white wax, thus giving an effect like marble.

The wax comes from petroleum: it is one of the materials left after gasoline, kerosene, and the other valuable liquid ingredients have been removed. Its use for candles occurred to people almost as soon as it was discovered. Dr James Young took out a patent for obtaining 'paraffin from bituminous shales' in 1850, and revolutionised the candle industry, which had been dependent on smelly tallow candles up to that time.

Although it is difficult to think of it in this way, when we see the enormous refineries and the complicated tracery of chemical plant used by oil companies, petroleum is a natural product. It is the result of thousands of years of underground heat and pressure applied to the fossil remains of the plants and trees that existed long before man and animals appeared on the scene. In the great earth movements and eruptions of that unsettled time whole areas of forest and jungle were buried and gradually turned into petroleum or coal, depending on the circumstances.

As petroleum is made from plants, it is a very complicated mixture of materials. Not only that, but the mixture varies from place to place, and the material from, say, a Texas oilfield is not the same as that from Russia or the Persian Gulf. After all, as now, different types of vegetation grew in different areas.

Just as the oil varies, so does the paraffin wax obtained from it. The wax is a mixture, and the components of the mixture (and thence the behaviour of the wax) vary according to the source of the wax and the type of refining treatment it has received.

Most oil companies separate the wax into about five grades, from *very soft wax*, which melts at around 110–112°F. (43–44°C.), through two grades of *soft wax* melting at 118–120°F. (48–49°C.) and 125–130°F. (52–54°C.), and two grades of *hard wax* melting at 130–135°F. (54–57°C.) and 135–140°F. (57–60°C.). The soft waxes are used mainly for cosmetics and ointments, for coating the wood of matches, and for making waxed papers for wrapping. Hard waxes are used for candles – details of the various grades and their specific uses are given below.

Paraffin wax is undoubtedly the cheapest wax in commercial use – hundreds of thousands of tons are made every year – and it gives a good light and is attractive in appearance. However, despite these advantages, it also has a number of dis-advantages. One of these is directly caused by the translucency of the material. When you hold up a piece of paraffin wax to the light, it looks bright, because you can see some light diffusing through it, but if you look at it with the light behind or above you, you will notice that it seems to be gray rather than white. If you hold a piece of white paper near it you will soon notice the difference. This is because the light goes through the wax and is not reflected from it. You find the same effect if you make a grease spot on a piece of paper – held up to the light it looks brighter than the paper, but when you look down at it the spot appears grayer.

In practice this means that candles made entirely from paraffin wax tend to look dull; the whites are not really white, and colours added to the wax get dulled down by the grayness of the basic wax shade.

Secondly, paraffin wax candles are rather difficult to remove from moulds, especially rigid moulds like metal. This is because the wax does not contract very much as it cools, and it also seems to have a tendency to stick to metal surfaces. This can cause disasters when you try to get a paraffin wax candle out of the mould: it is just as bad as a cake sticking in the cake tin.

Thirdly, even hard wax has a low melting-point, and it tends to soften in warm weather, so that the candles made from paraffin wax alone sag and warp when the sun comes out. James Young, who invented the use of the wax for candles, soon found out this disadvantage. He tried making tall altar candles, but soon found that they could sag over to an inverted U-shape distressingly easily when the candles round them were alight and thus warming the air. Fortunately it was soon discovered that various materials added to the wax, *stearin* in particular, will harden it and raise the melting-point, at the same time improving the other characteristics.

Paraffin wax is usually sold in large blocks or slabs, or flakes of the material packed in bags. The flakes are easier to melt, but usually more expensive than the block material. You can break up a block very easily in a number of ways – wrap it in paper and hit it sharply with a hammer, or warm a strong and fairly blunt knife in hot water or over the stove, and press it down firmly into the wax. This will cut a groove, and if you go on pressing down the block should soon split apart at this point. If not, reheat the knife and cut a little deeper. If you make it a rule to do all your candle-making operations on sheets of newspaper, you will easily be able to pick up any fragments that have split off and put them in your melting vessel with the main blocks.

If your supplier has a range of paraffin waxes, you may at first be confused about the right one to choose for your candles. In general hard wax with a melting-point of 130–135°F. is the most suitable for general use. Hard wax with a melting-point of 135–140°F. (57–60°C.) gives a very much firmer candle, and it tends to contract a little in the mould, thus overcoming one of the disadvantages of the material to some extent. However, it takes longer to melt, and when mixed with other waxes it may make a blend that does not melt easily in hot water. This is an important point, because most candle-making techniques depend on the use of a water-bath to melt the wax safely.

Soft wax with a melting-point of 125–130°F. (52–54°C.) is too soft for use in making whole candles, but it is sometimes useful for making special blends. For instance, if you want to make candles dipped in wax of a contrasting colour (see Chapter 3), it is often convenient to make the inner candle in hard wax, and the coloured coating in soft wax. Then the coating can be melted at a fairly low temperature and there is no danger of melting the inner candle and perhaps spoiling its shape.

In any case, paraffin wax, for nearly all candle-making purposes, should be blended with other materials to get over the basic disadvantages of the material. The most important blending agent is *stearin*.

Stearin

Stearin is another name for commercial stearic acid. The name may be a little confusing if you think of acids as corrosive, dangerous materials like nitric acid or hydrochloric acid. Stearin is chemically an acid, but it is quite harmless to touch, and will not damage clothes or surfaces. It behaves for most purposes exactly like beeswax or paraffin wax. Just remember, however, that when stearin is *hot* it can corrode metals just like other acids. If you drop melted stearin on a copper or iron saucepan, for example, it may leave a mark because it has eaten into the metal.

Plumbers use stearin or tallow to clean up lead before they joint pipes: this is because when it is heated it dissolves away scale on the lead and leaves a clean surface for the solder.

Pure stearic acid is a hard white crystalline material like beeswax, except that it has a very faint smell of tallow or hot fat about it. It is one of the most important components of tallow, suet, lard, and many vegetable oils. The pure material melts at 157°F. (69°C.) but when it is sold for candle making it is usually mixed with other fatty materials from tallow, and the melting-point is lower.

Stearin has a number of important uses in candle making. First, and possibly most important, it is harder and less easily softened by heat than paraffin wax, and therefore stearin added to the wax will make candles that can stand up in hot conditions without sagging.

Secondly, stearin added to wax makes a blend that contracts quite sharply as it cools. This means that the candles come away easily from the moulds. It also means that the wax tends to contract downwards from the top of the candle as it cools: as the outside of the candle cools before the centre, the depression forms as a kind of inverted cone round the wick which can be an inch or so deep with a large candle. You will find in the instructions for making candles in moulds (Chapter 4) that 'topping-up' is an important part of the process as the candle wax cools down, otherwise your candles will have holes in them at the top of the mould.

Stearin is also whiter and more opaque than paraffin wax. This overcomes the problems of grayness and dullness of the colours. If you mix enough stearin with your paraffin wax the whites will look much whiter and the colours brighter (this sounds like a detergent advertisement, but in this case all the claims are true!). You can get an interesting effect by coating a coloured wax candle with a thin layer of pure white stearin. This gives a muted, old-fashioned appearance to the design.

Stearin is also a better solvent for dyestuffs than paraffin wax, and it is usual to employ it to disperse the colours. If you buy wax ready-coloured, or colours in the form of dye blocks or tablets, they will be mixed with stearin already, but if you are using pure oil-soluble colours you will need stearin to dissolve them successfully.

For all these purposes you will find that about 10 per cent of stearin added to paraffin wax gives very good results. If you are using colours, dissolve these in the stearin and then mix the stearin with the wax. You will need to melt the stearin first, then melt the wax, and stir them together, using, according to the scale on which you are working, 1 lb. of stearin to 9 lbs. of wax or $1\frac{1}{2}$ ozs. of stearin to $14\frac{1}{2}$ ozs. of wax. A very rough guide, if you already have the materials melted, is that one tablespoon of stearin is added to every half pint of wax (use a little less than a tablespoonful if you are working in U.S. pints).

You can also make candles in pure stearin, or stearin blended with beeswax. These are more expensive than paraffin wax candles, but they are very hard and brilliant in colour. Strong contrasting colours like red and white show up very well with stearin candles.

The flame is smaller and hotter than with a paraffin wax candle, and because the stearin or stearin/beeswax mixture does not melt easily, the candle will burn longer. If you want a brighter light you may find it necessary to use a larger size of wick than you would calculate for a paraffin wax candle of the same diameter (see Table I, p. 85 for details of wick sizes and how to calculate them).

Most candle-makers' suppliers will provide a candle wax, in blocks or flakes, that consists of paraffin wax and stearin in the right proportions. You can usually get coloured waxes as well, although the range of shades may be restricted. Stearin itself is supplied in flakes or powder: used at 10 per cent, a pound or two will make a lot of candles.

Microcrystalline wax

Microcrystalline wax is another product of petroleum, and is extracted in similar ways to paraffin wax. As the name suggests, its crystals are very small, and the general appearance is that of a matt white, fairly hard solid. Some microcrystalline waxes are off-white to yellow in shade.

Like paraffin wax they come in a range of melting-points and hardness. Soft microcrystalline wax melts around 130–140°F. (54–60°C.) and is rather less brittle than paraffin wax. It is particularly useful for adding thin sheets of decoration to candles, or for making flat-faced candles with moulded relief on the faces.

Hard microcrystalline wax melts at fairly high temperatures, around 175–190°F. (79–88°C.) and is sometimes added to paraffin wax to improve mould release and to make a stronger candle. It can also be used for making chunky candles (see Chapter 4, page 45) where the higher melting-point of the microcrystalline wax is useful to prevent the chunks from melting when the background wax is poured on to them. They also show up rather better in this type of candle because the texture of the microcrystalline wax is different from that of the paraffin wax/stearin blend surrounding the chunks.

Spermaceti

This is a bright white crystalline wax which is extracted from the sperm whale. The enormous head cavities of that giant animal are filled with sperm oil, in which the spermaceti wax is dissolved or suspended as crystals that can be separated from the oil. No one quite knows what purpose this oil and wax in the whale's head serves in its life, but the value of the sperm oil and spermaceti has undoubtedly led to the death of many tens of thousands of whales in the enormous slaughter of the animals over the last few centuries.

The wax is hard and brittle and looks rather like stearin. Spermaceti has been used for candles since about the latter half of the eighteenth century. Before the use of paraffin wax was discovered spermaceti and beeswax were the only alternatives to tallow and kitchen fat for making candles. Spermaceti, though more expensive than tallow, was quite a lot cheaper than beeswax, gave a good light, and produced none of the unpleasant smells associated with tallow candles or dips, so spermaceti became the material for the better class of candle, except for very special occasions when beeswax was used. It is interesting to note that our modern unit for measuring illumination, the 'candle power', was originally based on the lighting power of a spermaceti candle of standard size and wick.

Spermaceti is too brittle to be used successfully for decorative candle making, so it is usual to add some other wax to it to increase the elasticity and flexibility. Beeswax is a useful ingredient for this purpose, and a combination of half spermaceti and half beeswax gives a very opaque, hard candle with a good steady light.

On the other hand, as the production of spermaceti involves the destruction of the sperm whale – an intelligent and harmless animal that is already over-hunted and in danger of extinction – it may be better to avoid its use for candles. Most of its properties can be reproduced with mixtures of other waxes.

Beeswax

The use of beeswax for making candles and dips, like the discovery of fire, is lost in the mists of prehistory. Attracted to bees' nests by the honey, it would not be long before early man discovered that the wax surrounding the honey burned with a bright light.

Beeswax is produced by worker bees: they eat about 10 lbs. of honey to produce 1 lb. of wax. It is a yellowish hard wax with a curious elasticity in its feel, and a characteristic and pleasant smell of honey. Beeswax straight from the hive tastes sweet and aromatic, but after it has been bleached it seems to lose most of its taste.

Beeswax candles have been known for centuries. There are mentions of them in ancient Roman writings, and many ancient temples must have been lighted with beeswax candles before they became such a feature of Christian churches.

Modern beeswax is extracted from the comb by draining off the honey, melting the combs in hot water, and straining off the impurities (cocoons, dead bees, etc.). The remaining mass is pressed hydraulically to give more wax of a lower quality which is used for polishes and so on. It melts at around 140°F. (60°C.), and is very tough and opaque, so that candles made from it are a striking creamy white and stand up well to handling, rolling, and so on. It takes oil-soluble colour very easily.

Beeswax is supplied in blocks that can be used to make whole candles, or added to paraffin wax to increase the opacity of the material. Beeswax also helps to increase the polish on the surface of a paraffin wax candle – about 10 per cent or even less will make a great improvement. The addition also makes paraffin wax candles burn more slowly and therefore last longer.

If you want to make pure beeswax candles you will find that it has one disadvantage: it tends to stick to rubber and metal moulds, unless you treat them with extra care beforehand. The simplest treatment is to rub the inside of the mould well with ordinary dishwashing liquid detergent, but special mould-release compounds are also available from some suppliers.

Beeswax is also supplied in sheets, often embossed with a hexagonal pattern like the cells in a beehive. This is for making rolled candles, a technique that is peculiar to beeswax because of its considerable elasticity compared with paraffin wax. Beeswax candles were traditionally rolled from sheets of the wax in medieval times, partly because it was difficult to make moulded candles with the material, and this craft has persisted to quite recent times for the production of votive and altar candles.

Often the finish on a beeswax candle rolled by an expert craftsman was almost as perfect as that of a moulded candle, but as it burned it was possible to see the spiral line running from the outside to the centre, that marked the layers of wax rolled into the cylindrical shape.

Pure beeswax candles, like stearin candles, need a rather larger and looser wick than paraffin wax candles, because the wax melts less easily and does not therefore creep up the fibres of the wick so readily.

17

Other waxes

Many other waxes and fats have been used for candles at various times, either for special effects or because these materials were more easily available at certain periods or places. None of them is particularly important for the modern candlemaker, but they are sometimes mentioned in older books and recipes, and it is as well to know what they are and how they may best be replaced with modern materials.

Ozokerite or *ceresin* was quite widely used at one period, especially in America. It is a hard white wax that occurs in large deposits in Utah and in some districts of Europe, notably Galicia in Poland. It is a petroleum type of material, but the deposits are unusual because they consist only of wax, with no liquid petroleum or natural gas, so it can be dug out of the ground practically ready for use. Ozokerite is the name for the natural wax simply filtered to remove dirt: ceresin is the same material bleached to give a slightly better colour.

Ozokerite melts at about 167–171°F. (75–77°C.) and is rather like a high-melting-point microcrystalline wax. Most of it is used for cosmetic purposes, being particularly useful for making lipsticks. Having a high melting-point it does not melt easily in hot weather or in brightly lighted store displays, while as it has very small crystals it does not have the 'grainy' feel of paraffin wax and similar materials.

If you find a recipe for candles that uses ozokerite or ceresin, and you want to try it out, you will probably get equally good results by using hard microcrystalline wax.

Carnauba Wax is a very hard wax that is obtained from the cera trees of South America. Most of it is used in floor and furniture polishes, where it gives hard wear and a high gloss. It is very expensive, mainly because the cera trees do not produce very much wax at a time – it takes about 40 million trees to produce the 11,000–12,000 tons of carnauba wax used annually.

In candles, it imparts great hardness and a high melting-point (the wax itself melts at about 186–192°F., 86–89°C.) and it was at one time employed for making candles specially for hot climates. A little carnauba wax added to the usual mixture of paraffin wax and stearin helped to stop the candles sagging in the heat. However, it is hard to get these days, and is also expensive. If you have a recipe using carnauba wax, you can replace it by using extra stearin or hard microcrystalline wax. For example, if your recipe calls for 5 per cent carnauba wax, put an extra 10 per cent of stearin in, and cut down the amount of paraffin wax accordingly.

Montan Wax is very similar to carnauba wax. It is made artificially by heat treatment of peat, and is used to replace carnauba wax in polishes (it melts at about 176–187°F., 80–86°C.) and can be used for hardening the wax mixtures of candles. However, if you cannot get hold of montan wax, it can be replaced by extra stearin or hard microcrystalline wax.

Ghedda Wax, *Insect Wax*, *Chinese Wax* are all names for waxes like beeswax that are obtained from various species of insect in China and the Pacific Islands. They are very similar to beeswax and may be replaced by it in candle wax mixtures.

Coconut Oil and Palm Kernel Oil at one time were used in candle mixtures. They are not really oils, because they are solid at most normal room temperatures, and are easily bleached to make a white waxy material that burns with a good light.

They melt at about 75°F. (24°C.). The main disadvantage of these fats is that they produce the 'burning fat' smell of acrolein (see page 12). On the other hand, the fats themselves possess a pleasant smell of coconut that is also released as the candles burn, and which must have been a great improvement on the smell of tallow candles or the early unrefined paraffin wax. Coconut oil can usually be obtained fairly easily from stores dealing in Oriental foods, as it is a popular cooking oil for preparing Indian food. Alternatively, coconut and palm kernel oils in recipes can be replaced by soft paraffin wax or soft microcrystalline wax.

Bayberry Wax and *Laurel Wax* are similar materials obtained from various species of myrtle and laurel tree, as a fatty coating round the fruit. They were used extensively in Europe in earlier centuries, and by the pioneers in America, because they smell pleasanter than tallow as they burn. While they tend to produce acrolein, they also have a pleasant smell of bay or myrtle.

Bayberry wax is rather hard to obtain and you may have to gather your own laurel or myrtle fruits and melt out the wax yourself. As the main attraction of the wax is its smell, don't spoil it by adding stearin or paraffin wax to harden it, use a good quality beeswax. If you find the wax mentioned in a recipe and can't get hold of any, coconut oil will give you the right consistency, although of course it has a different smell.

WICKS

A candle really works in the same way as an oil lamp. In both of them fuel is drawn up the fibres of the wick by capillary attraction, and burns there, spread out on the threads of the wick so that it has contact with the air. The only difference between the oil lamp and the candle is that the fuel in a candle is kept solid until just before it is needed. The heat of the flame melts a little pool of wax just around the wick, and it is this melted wax that flows to keep the flame going.

If you have used an oil lamp you will know that the wick needs careful adjustment. If the wick is too low it gets flooded with oil and the flame tends to go out easily. If the wick is too high the flame is large but a lot of smoke is produced. The same things happen with candle wicks. Obviously they cannot be adjusted like the wick in an oil lamp, but they can be regulated by choosing thick or thin wicks to suit the size of the candle and the type of wax that is being used.

For example, if you make a fairly large candle, say about 3 ins. diameter, and put a very small wick in it, you will find that soon after you have lighted the candle, the flame will splutter and go out. This is because the pool of melted wax is far more than the wick can carry easily to the flame, and the wick gets flooded. On the other hand, if you put a very thick wick into a narrow candle, you will find that the flame produces clouds of black smoke, because the wax is not melting fast enough to keep pace with the flow up the wick.

Waxes like stearin or beeswax, which have high melting-points, do not produce such a big pool of wax as paraffin wax or other low-melting-point materials tend to. To make these harder waxes burn smoothly, it is necessary to use a larger and looser wick to ensure a supply of melted wax to the flame.

Figure 1 shows the extreme positions for satisfactory performance of a wick. At one extreme, the wick is burning surrounded by a fairly wide and deep pool of

FIG. 1 The effects of wick size. The candle on the left has too large a wick, so that the flame is smoky and the wax is melting over the side of the bowl. The candle on the right has too small a wick, and not enough wax is getting to the flame to maintain burning.

melted wax – this is the common state of paraffin wax candles. If the wick is too small, this pool will swamp it and the flame will go out. If the wick is too large the pool will get bigger and bigger until at last the sides of the candle melt away and a cascade of wax goes down the side. Somewhere between these states is just right: the pool is small, but not so small that the candle smokes.

With stearin and beeswax candles the usual problem is that not enough wax is getting to the flame. Here the candle is burning with a 'clean bowl', not a pool. The wick and the flame are too small to give enough heat to melt the wax, while at the other extreme the candle is smoking because more wax is getting to the flame than can be burned completely. Again, somewhere in between these two states is just right.

All this goes to show that the wick is a most important part of the candle, and it must be chosen with great care. Fortunately wicks are produced in a number of different sizes and capacities, so that you can choose the right one.

Choosing a wick for your candle
In early times, before cotton was commonly available to make a wick, candles and dips were made with any fibrous material that was to hand. Pine branches were dipped in tallow to make torches – the turpentine in the pine wood itself helping

to give a brighter light. Rushlights were made by drying rushes and dipping them in tallow: the porous pith of the rushes served to carry the melted fat to the flame.

Soon people realised that threads were useful as candle wicks, and lengths of cord or threads from rope picked apart were used. *Flambeaux* and *links* were lengths of hemp obtained in this way, which were dipped in tallow to make crude candles. In the eighteenth century the links were used particularly for lighting the way in towns. 'Link-boys' guided travellers home through the dangerous and filthy streets with their flaring lights, and many old houses had their own cone-shaped metal extinguishers near the front door for the boys to put out their links once the journey was completed.

In the open air the smoke and smell of the links might have been tolerable, but in the houses themselves the hempen wicks produced great clouds of smoke that blackened the walls and ceilings and the clothes of the inhabitants as well. Cotton wicks, which were introduced late in the eighteenth century, were some improvement, but the candles still smoked, mainly because the burnt ends of the wicks tended to stick up straight in the flame, thus interfering with proper burning. These ends, or 'snuffs', could be cut off with candle-snuffers, little pairs of tongs or scissors specially made for the purpose, that often turn up in antique shops. They usually had a little cone-shaped end to douse the flame, a miniature of the larger cones used by the link-boys. But even so, keeping a candle burning brightly without smoke was almost impossible until *plaited wicks* were invented.

No one knows quite who thought of plaiting the cotton in wicks, instead of twisting it like ordinary thread or string. The plaited wick does not stick up in the flame. It curves over sideways and the end of the wick burns away in the edge of the flame, so that the wick is essentially 'self-snuffing'. All candle wicks are now plaited. If you try to make your candles with string or similar material for the wicks, you will find that you need the candle-snuffers fairly often to stop the candle flame smoking. Unless you want authentic eithteenth-century smokiness, always use the proper plaited wicks.

Nearly all wicks are plaited together in three bundles. The number of strands in the bundle decides the capacity of the wick. For example, a 3/10 wick is three bundles of 10 strands each plaited together, a 3/40 wick three bundles of 40 strands. Table I (p. 85) shows you the size of wick to select for various types and sizes of candle. Remember, however, that waxes vary, and you may have to modify these sizes a little one way or the other, so if you are working with a new shape or a new wax mixture, try one candle to check on the suitability of the wick before you make a batch of twenty!

FIG. 2 Candle snuffers. This is one of the traditional patterns. The scissor blades are to cut off the smoking wick, and the conical bowl fixed to one blade is to catch the wicks when they are cut off, and also to extinguish the candle when necessary.

Always remember the following points about candle wicks:

1. Choose the right size of wick for your candle. If you are working with candles of irregular shape, try to estimate the average diameter and choose a wick appropriate to this – use Table I or ask your supplier for a wick suitable for the average diameter.

2. If you are making cone-shaped candles, choose a wick that is right for a candle of one-third the diameter of the base. Remember that you will probably want to show off the candle to your friends in its complete state, so it is more important that it should burn at the right rate at the top than near the base.

3. If you want to make candles that burn down in the centre leaving a hollow (you will find instructions for these in various places in this book), use a wick that is smaller than the recommended size. For example, if you make a 3-in. paraffin wax/stearin candle and you want a hollow in the middle, use a 3/20 wick, not a 3/30. You will find that as the burning goes on, there is always the danger of the wicks becoming flooded in this type of candle, and it is not usually possible to make a hollow more than 5 ins. deep before this happens.

4. Always soak the wick in wax before you use it. Dip it in hot wax and pull it straight as the wax cools.

5. Never let water get on a wick unless it has been heavily waxed beforehand. Water stops wax from penetrating the threads, and this can cause irregular burning or spluttering of the flame. Some of the methods of candle making described in this book involve ice or water in contact with the wax. In these cases you will find that the instructions tell you to put a thick layer of wax on the wick before starting the other operations.

6. Ensure that the wick is always central in a candle, otherwise you will find that the candle burns lopsidedly and soon loses its shape.

7. In some of the methods described in this book, it is convenient to make up the wax shape before the wick is inserted. There are two ways of getting the wick in. Either drill a small hole with an ordinary hand drill and a small bit, or push a hot knitting-needle into the wax to make a hole, then push the wick in. You can buy lead-cored wick from candlemakers' suppliers. This stays much stiffer and is easy to insert.

8. You can also use lead-cored wicks for other candles, where they can be useful because they can be made to stand up without other support. Suppose, for instance, that you want to make a candle in a glass (see Chapter 7). You can make a self-supporting lead-cored wick by bending a circular base (see Figure 3 which is enlarged for clarity).

9. When preparing your candle for display, trim the wick to about $\frac{1}{2}$ in. Keep the burning area clean: bits of dead match or shreds of wick will clog the pool of wax and spoil the evenness of the flame.

10. Don't let your candles burn in a draught, otherwise you will find that one side of the candle burns down much faster than the other, and the shape will be spoiled.

11. When you extinguish a candle, push the wick into the pool of hot wax. This will stop it smouldering and smoking, and ensure that the wick is fully charged with wax for when you want to light the candle again.

12. Always be sure that candles are vertical when they burn, otherwise wax will rapidly drip down one side and melt away a channel.

13. If you still have trouble with smoking or irregular burning of your candles, consult the Fault Chart in Chapter 8.

COLOURS

A great deal of the charm of candles comes from the combination of the brightness and translucency of the wax, and the glow of the flame. However, not many candle-makers would care to work exclusively in white wax, and colours are as important as the wax mixtures.

Dyes for wax are different from those used for textiles, because they have to be soluble in the wax. Not many ordinary dyestuffs are suitable for wax or oil for they tend to remain in clumps or spots instead of dispersing completely to an even colour. You can make up your coloured wax, in emergency, by using coloured wax crayons added to the mix, but this is expensive and unsatisfactory compared with the use of the proper wax dyes.

If you want to make up your coloured waxes direct from the dyestuffs, suitable materials are as follows:

Reds: Eosin (bright bluish pink), Rose Bengal.
Orange: Sudan IV.
Yellows: Tartrazine (lemon-yellow), Auramine (orange-yellow).
Greens: Brilliant Green, Oleate Green.
Blue: Induline.
Violet: Methyl Violet.
Black: Oil Black.

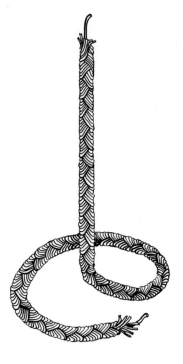

FIG. 3 A free-standing wick made with lead-stiffened wicking. This is drawn very much magnified to show how to make the wick stand up.

Many dyestuff suppliers will have alternative lists of suitable oil-soluble dyes. The only difficulty you may have with such suppliers is that their *minimum* order for any particular dyestuff will probably be enough to make about ten million candles! Fortunately most suppliers of candlemakers' equipment can sell you dyestuffs by the ounce or in similar small quantities.

Be careful when you are handling these concentrated dyes. They are extremely powerful colours, and can easily stain your hands and other surfaces. Eosin, in particular, is the dyestuff that is put into lipsticks to make them indelible and 'kiss-proof', so you can guess that stains from this dye are going to be troublesome to remove. Don't let the dyestuffs lie around if you spill any – wipe them up immediately – and avoid handling them on plastic surfaces, because many plastics are permanently dyed quite easily.

Even although they are oil-soluble, these dyes do not disperse easily in paraffin wax. It is best to dissolve them in stearin or beeswax (depending on the mixture of waxes that you want to use), and then add this to the paraffin wax in the right proportions.

It must be realised that even as little as an ounce of some of these dyes will colour several hundred pounds of wax, so you only need to disperse it in tiny pinches. An alternative that is far more satisfactory for most candlemakers is to buy the colours already dispersed in stearin, and made into discs or tablets of standard weight. For example, many suppliers stock coloured discs that will make up 4 lbs. of wax. If you want lighter shades you can use half a disc, or dissolve the disc in a larger quantity of white wax blend. This is not only a cleaner and safer process than working with the pure dyestuffs, but it ensures that you can always reproduce any shade that you wish.

Unless you are working with very large amounts of wax, the pure colours have to be measured out in thousandths of an ounce, and you are unlikely to be able to repeat the exact amount unless you have an analytical chemist's balance. With the stearin discs, however, you know that one disc in, say, 5 lbs. of wax, will always make the same shade.

A third alternative that suits many workers is to buy the wax blend already coloured. This is fine if the particular wax blend made up by your supplier suits your methods of working. You can make new colours by mixing the waxes in various proportions, although you may find that some of the results are rather dull. This is because very few of the dyestuffs are pure colours – pure red and pure yellow will make orange, but if you have a slightly bluish red and a slightly greenish yellow the result of mixing them will definitely be more brown than orange.

Don't put too much colour into your blends, when you make them yourself. Over-dyed wax does not glow so well when the candle is lighted.

PERFUMES

You can add perfumes to candles, and the fragrance will be distributed in the room as the candle burns.

Ordinary perfumes and toilet waters are not suitable for this because they are almost invariably made up with alcohol, which does not mix with paraffin wax. You need special oil-based perfumes. Fortunately these are made up for other

PLATE I   Dipped candles. The two centre ones have been rolled and twisted.

PLATE 2 The candle at the back has been dipped in successive layers of colour, then carved back. The others are made with metal moulds.

purposes (perfuming hairdressing, and so on) and they are usually available from candlemakers' suppliers. Delicate fragrances are not really appropriate in candles. Choose fairly full-bodied perfumes like sandalwood, amber, heliotrope, patchouli, and so on.

Half a fluid ounce of perfume is quite enough for 20 lbs. of wax, unless you want a powerful joss-stick effect, so you can be economical with your perfumes. If you add the perfume to the hot wax, do this *just* before pouring, otherwise perfume ingredients will evaporate and be lost before your candle is made.

Alternatively you can add the perfume by soaking the wick in it before you fit the wick into the mould. This is a useful method if you are making multicoloured candles or similar products that involve melting a lot of small quantities of wax; it is far less trouble than adding a drop or two of perfume to every batch of wax.

Chapter 2

Equipment

Candles can be made in any kitchen with ordinary kitchen utensils, and this simplicity of equipment is one of the attractions of the craft. Many people make very effective and professional-looking candles with nothing more complicated than a saucepan, a jug, and a few oddments like old table knives. All you need in the way of materials can be bought in very convenient and easy-to-use forms from the various candlemakers' suppliers, and all you have to provide is the minimum of equipment plus your own care and patience to get good results.

However, there are a few pieces of inexpensive extra equipment that will make your craft easier or more successful, and these will be mentioned in this chapter where they are appropriate.

The basic process of candle making is in four stages: melting the wax, pouring the wax into moulds or over wicks, cooling the finished candles, and applying any special finishing processes that you want to carry out. Of these stages the actual melting requires the most care, because, as you will see in the chapters that follow, many successful effects depend on getting the wax to the right temperature before you shape it into candles.

It will therefore pay you to get a *thermometer*. This does not have to be very accurate – none of the temperatures given in this book are meant to be taken as any more than a guide, and if you can keep your waxes within about 2–3° either side of the figures mentioned, you will be working quite precisely enough. The temperatures that are mostly important in melting wax are in the range 150° and 210°F. (66–99°C.), but occasionally you need to work at higher temperatures (for example, in making sand-moulded candles, see page 53), so choose a thermometer with a range that includes the whole scale from room temperature to about 400°F. (205°C.). A sugar-boiling thermometer, as used for making candy, is quite suitable, and will have the right sort of robust construction to save it from damage as you poke it about in the hot wax. Alternatively you can buy a special thermometer from candlemakers' suppliers (although you will probably find that this turns out to be a sugar-boiling thermometer, anyway).

Don't use your thermometer to stir wax – a wooden or metal spoon is much better for the purpose, and costs far less. Plastic spoons are not suitable for wax melting, they will almost certainly soften in the hot wax, and may melt altogether. When your thermometer gets covered with wax, as it will whenever you dip it into the wax mixture, don't try to pick the pieces of wax off – you are more likely to break the glass of the thermometer. Hold it under the hot tap until the wax melts away.

26

Try to keep your thermometer somewhere safe, not jumbled up in a drawer full of tools. Sugar-boiling thermometers are quite strong, but an unlucky tap on the glass with a heavy knife handle can ruin them.

Melting equipment for wax
Most waxes used in candle making can easily be melted below the boiling-point of water, so they can be handled safely and conveniently by putting the container of wax in hot water in a saucepan or boiler. You will find that only once in this book is a method described that requires direct heating of the wax over the stove, and apart from this you should avoid putting your wax containers directly on an electric ring or flame. Candle wax is inflammable (it would not be much use for making candles if it were not!).

At the end of this chapter you will find a section on precautions against fire and burns or scalds. READ IT CAREFULLY BEFORE YOU EMBARK ON CANDLE MAKING. This is not to say that the craft is dangerous. The precautions are very simple and very commonsense, and there is no more danger in making candles than in frying potatoes – probably less.

The simplest melting equipment is a saucepan of water. Your wax can go in any convenient containers – old cups or mugs, food cans that have been carefully cleaned and dried, or jugs. Plastic vessels are not really suitable, because they tend to soften too much in the hot water and may actually melt or burn on the bottom of the saucepan, and metal vessels are liable to corrode slightly, especially if you are using wax blends with the addition of stearin. Food cans can be thrown away if they get corroded.

Many techniques call for a variety of colours of wax to be melted simultaneously, so try to get the biggest saucepan you can, so that all your cups or cans will fit in. You can often find the old-fashioned type of saucepan or boiler that was made for the large familes of earlier times, or a piece of equipment discarded from a restaurant or school kitchen, which will give you ample room for several wax containers.

Take a look from time to time when you are melting your wax, to make sure that there is still water in the saucepan, and that it has not boiled away. It is very easy in the interest of making a complex candle design to forget the humble melting-pot. Don't let water get into your wax: it will cause your candles to splutter and spit as they burn. Have a heavy cloth or oven glove to lift the wax containers out of the saucepan, because the human skin can only stand temperatures up to about 140°F. (60°C.) and most melting temperatures are beyond this. Always remember to pour your waxes well away from the stove, and do not be tempted to bring the moulds to the wax, otherwise you may start a fire by spilling wax on the heater.

Some candles are made by dipping (see pp. 32–38) and require a vessel for the wax that is rather longer than the finished candle, and which can be kept hot. If you make candles 1 ft. long, this can be difficult, because not many saucepans are as deep as this.

You can overcome this difficulty to a large extent by using a tall jug standing in a saucepan of hot water. Keep the water a good deal hotter than the temperature recommended for the wax, because obviously some of the heat will have to rise in the jug to melt the wax all through uniformly, but the method usually works well.

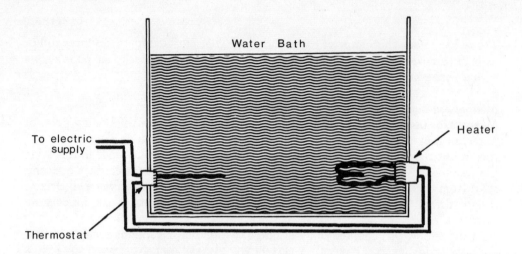

FIG. 4 Thermostatically controlled water bath for melting wax. The thermostat comes into the circuit between the supply and the tank heater, and switches the heater on or off as the temperature falls or rises.

The alternative is to find a metal pail or similar vessel that is at least 1 ft. deep, and can be used on the stove. If you can get hold of such a vessel, keep it for your candle work and don't let other members of the family use it for a general-purpose bucket.

When you are measuring the temperature of wax, especially if it is in the kind of container that is taller than your saucepan or water bath, remember to stir the wax first so that you get a true average temperature, not just the figure for the top or the bottom of the container, and take the temperature of the *wax*, not the surrounding water. The hot water may have to be several degrees higher than the wax because of heat losses, and quite often the water in a saucepan can be at about 210°F. while the wax is still only at 190°F. This is worth mentioning because some people tend to measure the temperature of the water rather than the wax to avoid having to clean the thermometer afterwards.

Some methods of dipping require lengths of tube to hold the wax, with no bottom in them, so that the wax is just floating on the surface of hot water. Lengths of plastic water pipe as used for drainage from gutters are ideal for this purpose, and should be available from builders' merchants for a very small sum. However, they do have the disadvantage that they float in water and therefore tend to tip over unless they are held down. If you can procure some lengths of metal drainpipe these will save you a lot of trouble. Some buildings have aluminium or zinc drainpipes – if you can find some of this, even from a demolished house, you can easily cut it into suitable lengths with a hacksaw.

For your melting vessel, if you can find the type of boiler that has its own heating element, of course you can make a magnificent piece of equipment. Sometimes these are used in catering for making coffee and tea, and you may be able to pick one up from a supplier of used catering equipment. This will get you right away from the kitchen stove, and you can melt your wax wherever it is convenient to

28

carry out your candle making. As an improvement to this, a thermostat can be added (unless the equipment has one already). This is fitted into the boiler and wired up between the electricity supply and the heating element. You can set the thermostat to any temperature, and it will maintain this temperature in the water in the vessel, by turning on the power when the water cools below the set temperature, and then turning it off again when the water gets hotter than the required temperature (see Figure 4).

The type of thermostat that is sold for control of home central-heating systems is no use for this application to candle-wax melting, because the range of temperature over which it works is too low – these thermostats being usually set for around 50–70°F. (10–21°C.) or a little higher. However, there are thermostats that are made for domestic water heating, immersion heaters and boilers, and so on, that are quite suitable and not very expensive. Look for a thermostat that operates between 120° and 210°F. (49–99°C.).

Don't start on this construction project yourself unless you have some experience of home electrical work, the combination of electricity and water can be dangerous unless you know what you are doing. Maybe if you can find a boiler or discarded coffee machine at a reasonable price, you can take it to a local handyman and get him to fit a thermostat while also explaining the range of temperatures you want to cover.

Once equipped with a water-bath of this type with thermostatic control, you may begin to wonder how you ever managed without it, because you can set the thermostat with confidence that your wax will not overheat, nor be too cold however long you take in setting up your other equipment.

Stands and clamps

Quite a number of operations in candle making require that moulds, pieces of pipe, and other bits of equipment are held still in a certain position while you pour wax into them, and then they need to be held in place until the wax cools. For instance, in Chapter 4 you will find directions for making candles in moulds held at certain angles, and it can be a very tedious business if you are standing holding a mould at an angle and praying for the wax to set solid *soon*.

There is a simple piece of equipment that is ideal for all these holding jobs – a laboratory retort stand and clamp (see Figure 5). The clamp is like a pair of tongs that can be tightened up by a screw, and the jaws can be used to hold moulds, or wicks, or almost anything else. The clamp itself can be adjusted at any angle by the connection to the stand. These stands and clamps can be obtained from chemical suppliers and some other sources, and they are not expensive considering how very useful they can be – just like a third hand, in fact.

Cooling

Many candles come out better if they are cooled fairly quickly, so a container of cold water is a good thing to have around when you are working. The ordinary plastic bucket is ideal for this.

FIG. 5 Laboratory stand and clamp. The clamp can
be fixed at any height on the stand and at any
angle, by adjusting the screws on the metal 'boss'
that fixes it to the stand.

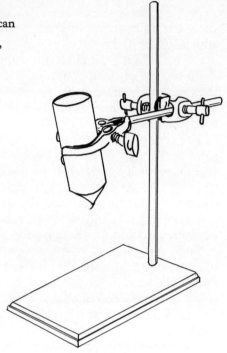

Other equipment

Other equipment for candle making is very simple. You need a good flat surface
to work on, and preferably one that is not affected by hot wax. Don't make your
candles on a polished table! Any strong table or bench will do. If you can get a sheet
of thick window glass or plate glass, about 2 ft. square, this is useful for making
sheets of wax for certain projects.

Spread newspaper over the surface when you are working, then you can always
pick up any wax that gets spilled or flakes off from the candles, and if you are
working with wax in block form you can spread newspaper underneath it when you
break it up to catch the little flakes that always fall away.

One thing that you need for most candle-making operations is a really sharp
knife for cutting candles square at the base, making up blocks of wax, and dozens of
other purposes. A good general-purpose craft knife with replaceable blades is a
worthwhile investment. You will also need scissors for cutting wicks and jobs like
that. Have a block of wood handy to do your cutting on, then you won't spoil the
surface of your working table.

A wicking needle is a useful tool for pushing wicks through flexible moulds – it
has a large eye that will take even thick pieces of wick. You can buy these from
candlemakers' suppliers, when you buy your lengths of wick, or if you have difficulty with this, look around in sewing stores for a bodkin or darning needle with a
large eye.

For decorating candles, you will find a number of methods described in the
chapters that follow that involve simple artists' tools. Lino-cutting tools can be

used to engrave designs in wax (see Chapter 6), and the methods used in batik work are often useful for applying coloured wax to candles. You will find instructions, for example, for using batik brushes and tjantings (batik pens) for drawing designs in hot wax. These simple tools are easily available from craft stores – in fact, many candlemakers' suppliers also deal in batik supplies.

PRECAUTIONS AGAINST FIRE AND BURNS

As I have said, making candles is no more dangerous than frying potatoes, but there are certain precautions that every candlemaker should take to avoid accidents. These are simply commonsense, but it is as well to list them. A wax fire is not only dangerous, but because burning wax gives off clouds of soot, quite a small fire can cause a lot of damage to home decorations.

1. As far as possible, never heat wax over a flame or hot electric ring, unless you have some type of double-boiler with water in it. Even a saucepan of water is adequate. There is one method in this book (Sand-moulding, Chapter 4) that involves direct heating of wax, but otherwise always have water between the heat and the wax.

2. Make sure your saucepan or boiler does not boil dry.

3. Always handle containers of wax with a glove or a thick cloth over your hand, when the wax is melted. Remember that wax does not *look* hot even when it is at the temperature of boiling water, and if you spill it on your hands it has an unpleasant habit of sticking to the skin, so that the burn is worse.

The same applies whether you are handling pots or cans of melted wax ready to pour, or moulds that you have just filled. If a mould tips over and spills all its hot wax, let it go. Don't try to catch it. It is far less likely to do any damage to the table or the floor than it is to burn your hands if you try to stop it falling.

4. If you have to heat wax directly over the stove, never let it get hotter than 350°F. (177°C.). Use your thermometer constantly during the heating stage. When the wax is hot enough for pouring, *turn off the stove* before you move the container of wax at all.

5. If wax does catch fire by accident, never try to put it out with water. This will just spread the burning wax, and if it is very hot it may splash back at you and burn you badly. Cover it. If you are working in a saucepan, put the saucepan lid over it, or wet a towel and throw this over the burning wax.

6. When you are burning your candles, always have something under them to catch drips. If you use candles as lighting at a party or barbecue, be very careful where you place them – remember that people have been very badly burned when dresses have caught fire from candles.

Chapter 3

Hand-made candles

Paraffin wax and other candle-making waxes have a fascinating range of consistencies and textures, as the temperature changes. They do not melt suddenly from hard solids to flowing liquids, like ice melting into water, but go through stages of softening where it is difficult to say whether they are soft solids or very thick liquids. If you melt a piece of candle wax and let it cool again, you will find that it stays soft and malleable for a long time, and it can still be shaped and moulded even when it has cooled almost to blood heat. This plastic stage allows the candlemaker to model the wax quite comfortably in the bare hands, and it also ensures that layers of wax can be 'welded' to one another without cracks or gaps, if they are heated to the softening stage.

Dipped candles
The simplest way of making candles is the oldest way – dipping. All you need in the way of apparatus is a jug or long pot a little taller than the length of the finished candle. Stand this in your water bath or in a large saucepan of water, and heat up

FIG. 6 Dipping candles. This is the simplest method. The wax is melted in a tall jug or pitcher and the wick is tied to a stick or pencil and dipped into the wax until it gets a good coating. The jug or pitcher can be heated in a saucepan of hot water (not shown).

enough plain white candle wax nearly to fill the jug. Maintain the temperature at around 180°F. (82°C.).

First wax the wick. Take a length of wick 2 or 3 ins. longer than the candle you want to make, and dip it in the melted wax. Pull it out and stretch it straight between your hands until the wax sets and the wick is stiff. Then tie it to a convenient handle – a small length of stick or even a fork will do. Dip the end of the wick in the hot wax to soften the wax at the tying end. Then simply lower the wick into the hot wax, let it stay in for about five seconds, and pull it out again. Hold it up for about thirty seconds, which will allow the wax to harden slightly, and then dip it again. and so on until the candle is as thick as you want it. If it shows signs of curving or warping, pull it straight gently between your hands. You will find that it is quite plastic in consistency. Then hang up the finished candle to cool, trim the wick and cut the base straight with a sharp knife.

You can make several candles simultaneously if you tie a series of wicks to a stick and dip them together (see Figure 7). This was the way in which the tallow chandlers made candles in medieval times. With practice you can make candles that are so straight and uniform in thickness that they look like a machine-made product.

Now try producing more interesting shapes. If you start off with a straight candle, fairly thin, and only dip it up to half its height, you can gradually build up a pear-shaped candle. You will find that it pays to rotate the candle slowly as you immerse it in the hot wax, so as to get an even coating of wax in each new layer, otherwise your candle may be lopsided. If you leave enough wick at each end to hold the candle, you can dip each end successively, while leaving the middle of the candle slim, and thus make an hour-glass shape (see Figure 8). Again, a little practice will soon show you how to get the wax built up exactly as you want it. If you get an unwanted bulge, pare off some of the wax carefully with a knife while it is still fairly

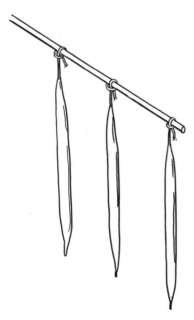

FIG. 7 Dipping several candles simultaneously. This method was used for centuries for the commercial production of candles.

FIG. 8 Shaped dipped candles. Candles do not have to be the same diameter from top to bottom – you can vary the thickness of the wax by dipping some parts more than others, and moulding the wax in your hands.

soft, then rotate the candle round in the hot wax to even up the surface and melt out the marks of the knife. You will find that the wax is so soft, for several minutes after dipping, that it will easily mark with the fingers. If you want a smooth candle, therefore, always hold it by the wick. On the other hand, you can make some interesting shapes by simple modelling of the surface between your hands. Warm wax is almost as easy to shape as clay or Plasticine.

If you want a square candle, you can make one by dipping an ordinary candle until you have a fairly fat cylinder, then cut down the sides smoothly with a knife or a heated blade of a palette knife.

Twisted candles
Candles twisted like barley sugar sticks are one of the oldest traditional decorative shapes. Commercial ones are usually made in moulds, but you can easily make twisted candles yourself purely by hand.

Take a candle made by dipping, and around $1\frac{1}{2}$ ins. in diameter. Use it while it is still fairly soft. Lay it on a clean flat surface like a piece of smooth wood or a plastic table top, and roll it with a rolling-pin or an empty bottle, taking care not to let the candle stick to the surface. If this should happen, you can slide a palette knife gently under the candle to release it, and turn it over. At intervals, tap the sides of the candle on the flat surface to square them off.

When the candle is fairly flat and wide, pick it up by the ends and gently but firmly twist these in opposite directions. You should have no trouble in getting an even twist all the way along. When the shape is right, plunge the candle into cold water and hold it there for at least five minutes to set. At first you will need to keep it in your hands to correct any slight distortions, but as it gets colder you can just put it down gently in the bottom of your bowl or bucket containing the cold water. Leave it there until it is entirely cold. Remember that wax holds the heat for a long time and the centre may still be soft even when the outside has set, so if you take it out too soon it will warp. Cut the base straight with a sharp knife and trim the wick to finish the candle.

34

FIG. 9 Twisted candles. These look very effective if you dip candles in three different colours.

Colour dipping

Dipped candles often look more attractive if they are given a final coat of coloured wax. Of course you can make dipped candles entirely of dyed wax, but you will find that a white candle with colour on top looks brighter, and when it burns the colour will glow more because more light can get through the middle of the candle and shine out through the thin coloured layer.

To colour-dip candles you can use a jug or pot similar to that used in making the basic dipped candle, and fill it with coloured wax. This is the best way to proceed if you want to dip a lot of candles in the same colour. Remember not to fill the container *too* full if your candles are rather fat, because they will displace a certain amount of wax and raise the level. Heat the water bath or saucepan to 180°F. (82°C.), dip your white candles in the coloured wax once or twice to get a good coating, then raise the temperature a little, to about 200°F. (93°C.) for a final dip, and lower the candle immediately into cold water. You will find that the hot dip at the end does not put on very much more wax, but it smooths the coating and gives a fine glossy finish.

If you are only making one or two coated candles with each colour, there is a more economical technique that is useful. All you need for this is a length of piping – plastic rainwater pipe is ideal – a little larger in diameter than your fattest candle and a few inches longer than the deepest dip you want to make. Fix this upright in a water-bath or deep saucepan, or even in a tall jug standing in a saucepan, and

35

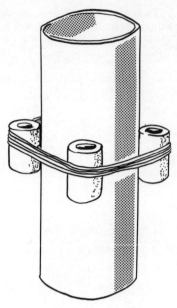

FIG. 10 Holding down plastic pipe. Plastic pipe is ideal material for dipping candles and similar jobs, but it has the disadvantage that it floats in water. If you tie pieces of lead pipe or any other heavy bits of metal round the pipe it will stay in place.

fill up with water until the level is about 4–5 ins. below the top of the pipe. You may have trouble in keeping the pipe upright if it is plastic, because this material tends to float and tip over. You can weight it or clamp it into position (an easy way to weight a length of pipe is to get some pieces of lead, brass, or other heavy metal – not iron, because it will rust) and tie these to the outside of the pipe by a string running round (see Figure 10). If you can get a laboratory stand and large clamp this is the ideal way of holding the pipe in position.

Now heat the water to about 180°F. (82°C.) and float coloured wax on to the surface of the water in the pipe until you have a layer about 1½ ins. deep. Make sure that there is enough room above the wax to allow for the displacement when you dip your candle. Take a white candle and lower it into the pipe right down into the wax layer, and then pull it steadily out again. Leave it for thirty seconds to set a little and then repeat the process if necessary. Now heat up the water until the wax layer is at about 200°F. (93°C.) and give your candle the final dip, plunging it immediately into cold water to set.

This method depends on the fact that wax floats on water, and also on the fact that a candle is not damaged by being dipped into water as long as the wick is well covered with wax. Don't try to use this method for the basic dipping of the candle, or your candle wick will get wet and the burning of the candle will be affected. If you have a large enough container and several lengths of piping you can keep several colours ready for dipping simultaneously, which makes possible a number of interesting variations on the standard colour-dipped candle.

Multiple twisted candles
Have ready three dipped candles of about the same size in plain white wax. These need not have been freshly prepared, although the twisting is easier if they are fairly soft. Choose three colours that will go together well, and float these in three

36

lengths of pipe in your water bath or saucepan. If the dipped candles have been freshly made and are fairly soft and malleable, heat the water to 180°F. (82°C.): if they are hard and set, heat the water to about 190°F. (88°C.). This will soften them sufficiently during the dipping stages.

If your colours are, say, red, green and yellow, dip one candle in the red wax and hang it up by its wick. If you tie loops in the top of the wicks and have hooks or nails handy, this saves a lot of trouble. Now dip the second candle in the green wax and hang it up. Finally, dip the third candle in the yellow wax. Carry on in rotation in this way until the colour layers look right, then heat the water up to 200°F. (93°C.) and give each candle its final dip, putting them into cold water as they are finished but not leaving them in the water for more than about twenty seconds. Take them out of the water and twist them together gently, pulling out the tops so that they point up vertically from the twisted portion. Leave the candles to harden thoroughly, cut the base flat, and trim the wicks. You will find that candles of about ¾–1 in. diameter give the best effect: thinner ones look spindly, while fatter ones are difficult to twist together.

If the candles show signs of hardening before you have finished you can soften them again to a certain extent by warming the whole assembly in a bowl of water at about 130°F. (54°C.) which is not too hot for your hands, but should just about soften the wax sufficiently for you to finish your twisting successfully.

Plaited candles
An elaboration on the twisted look is to take three candles in contrasting colours and actually plait them together. They need to be quite long and thin to make an effective plait (see Figure 11) and you will probably find that it helps to have someone else to hold the ends of the candles while you do the plaiting. Here again, if the candles harden up too much before you have finished, dip them in water at about 130°F. (54°C.).

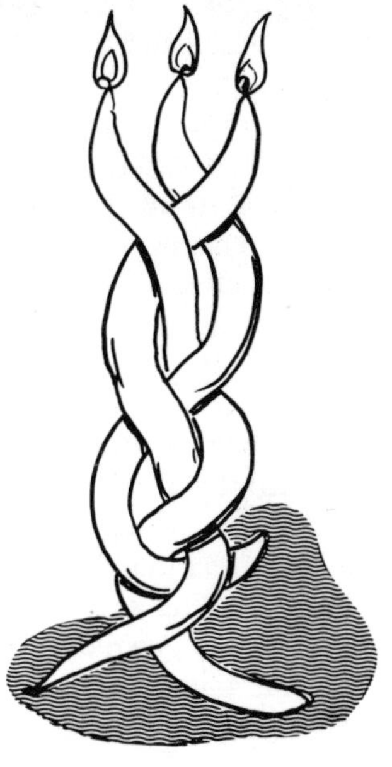

FIG. 11 Plaiting candles. This again looks good if you use candles in contrasting colours.

Rolling coloured candles

You will find that it is possible to roll, twist, and otherwise shape candles that have been coloured by dipping. In fact, this is the best way to make coloured twisted candles.

If you try to dip twisted candles after you have shaped them, there is a tendency for the candles to warp, and it is also rather difficult to get the colour to flow on evenly.

Use of softer coating waxes

In all these dipping methods, it is worthwhile to experiment with the use of softer waxes for the outer coloured layer. You can buy soft paraffin wax, with a melting-point in the 125–130°F. (52–54°C.) range, from most candlemakers' suppliers, and this can be coloured and used for dipping. The advantage is that they do not need such a high temperature of the water when you are dipping, and therefore there is less chance of spoiling the shape of the basic candle. They can also be finished off to a smoother surface, and are more easily modelled with the hands. Such waxes are very useful for multilayered candles.

Multilayered Candles

If you have a number of colours suitable for dipping, you can obtain a very interesting effect by putting different colours in successive layers on the same candle. Start off with a white dipped candle – a short stubby shape is best, spheres, pear-shapes, hour-glasses and so on, rather than long thin candles. Dip this in coloured wax, say a dark red, and carry on dipping in the usual way until you have about $\frac{1}{4}$ in. coating on the candle. Now wait thirty seconds and give it a further coat of another colour, perhaps bright green, and again build this up to about $\frac{1}{4}$ in. thick. If you find that it tends to lose shape, mould it in your hands between dippings. Now put on another colour, say yellow, in the same way, and finish off with a final coat. Dark colours like a rich blue look effective.

At this point your candle looks rather plain and dull, but you can transform it by carving out portions of the wax with a sharp knife, so that the brilliant colours inside show up like strata in a geological model; according to the depth to which you carve you can show all the colours or just one or two of them. Try the effects of holes of various shapes and sizes. If you carve them in the shapes of eyes and mouths you can get the effect of primitive masks (see Plate 2).

Intaglio work

Another effect you can achieve with multilayered candles is *intaglio* carving. For instance, an effective dice candle was made by dipping a short fat candle from white wax until it was practically spherical, and then carefully cutting it to a cube with a sharp knife, taking care not to damage the wick. This was then repeatedly dipped in black wax to give a layer about $\frac{3}{8}$ in. thick, and the cube shape was made sharper by smoothing and cutting with a knife to square off the corners. Finally this black cube was given a $\frac{1}{4}$-in. coat of white wax.

To make the outer white coating as opaque as possible, it was blended from paraffin wax with 10 per cent of white beeswax and 10 per cent of stearin.

When the white coat was cool but not entirely hard, the white outer layer was cut away in circular holes, so as to display the black wax underneath and make the spots on the dice. You can make the spots even by marking them out with the end of a circular piece of metal piping, or any circular object of the right size, and then cutting carefully round the marks with a sharp knife and lifting off the white wax. Be careful not to go too deep.

You can use this intaglio method for all kinds of designs, cutting out geometrical shapes, or letters, or even silhouette pictures, and you can, of course, have different colour schemes. If you have white wax inside and black or coloured wax outside you can achieve effects like the Grecian vases or the similar patterns as used in Wedgwood china.

If you do not want to take the trouble to shape the inside cube by hand, you can, of course, mould it in a suitable container. The next chapter will tell you all about methods with moulds.

Chapter 4

Moulds

Dipping, pouring, hand-shaping, and similar techniques will have taught you a lot about the way that candle waxes behave when heated and cooled, how easily the wax can be shaped and sculpted, and how bright and smooth the finish can be when you have mastered the art of adjusting the temperatures correctly. If you have any ambitions as a sculptor you will find that wax is the ideal medium for all kinds of artistic effects.

However, sooner or later every candlemaker wants to produce something more elaborate than can be done with hand methods, or you may want to produce three, four or a dozen candles that are strictly identical, for a decorative scheme, a large table at a barbecue, or something similar. It is at this point that moulds become necessary.

Wax is very easy to mould into shape. It is naturally slippery, so that quite often no extra lubricant is necessary to release it from the mould, and if the wax mixture is properly formulated it will contract slightly as it cools, so that the candle tends to come away from the mould surface on its own. Stearin added to the paraffin wax helps to produce this contraction, which is one of the reasons for including it in the mix: a small amount of beeswax added to the mixture, say about $\frac{1}{2}$–1 oz. per pound of paraffin wax, also helps to make the candles come away cleanly from the mould, and also makes them easier to polish and finish afterwards.

READY-MADE MOULDS

Most candlemakers' suppliers and craft shops can supply a range of moulds ready for use. These are usually in rubber, silicone rubber, or metal. If you are moulding candles for the first time you will find rubber moulds easier to handle. Choose one that looks attractive to you, not too big and not too small (about 2–2$\frac{1}{2}$ ins. diameter is about right for a first effort), and for your early attempts work with wax in one colour only – then if things go wrong you can just remelt and start again!

Choose a wick to suit the diameter of your mould (the supplier will advise you about this, or see Table I on page 85), and dip the wick in hot wax, pulling it straight as it cools. Then thread the waxed wick through the eye of a wicking needle, or any needle with a large eye, and push the needle through the top of the mould, making sure that the wick is central. Draw through about an inch of wick, and seal the hole, if necessary, with mould seal or modelling clay (or anything that is leak-proof and not affected by the hot wax).

Tie the other end of the wick to a piece of stick or plastic rod so that it can be

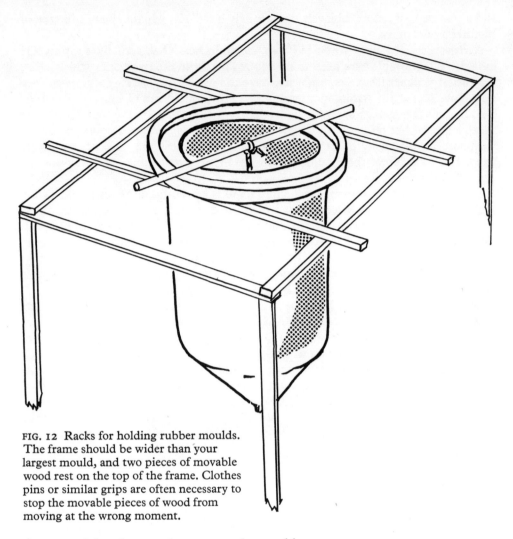

FIG. 12 Racks for holding rubber moulds.
The frame should be wider than your
largest mould, and two pieces of movable
wood rest on the top of the frame. Clothes
pins or similar grips are often necessary to
stop the movable pieces of wood from
moving at the wrong moment.

drawn straight when you have set up the mould.

Now arrange a rack to hold up the mould and the wick. There are two points to
be watched here. First, the mould must have space around it for air to circulate, so
that the wax cools properly, and second, nothing must distort the mould. Make
sure, for example, that the end of the wick is not resting on the table, or your candle
will have a misshapen end, and don't try to speed up the cooling stage by putting
your mould in a bath of cold water – the pressure of the water will just make the
sides of the mould cave in, and you will end up with a very odd-shaped candle.

A simple type of rack is shown in Figure 12. This consists of two parallel fixed
rods of wood, held about 6 ins. apart, and about 2 ft. up from the base. (Of course, if
your ambition is to make 6-ft. altar candles, you will have to make a correspondingly
larger rack to hold the moulds, but for most purposes 2 ft. is quite enough.) Half-
in. dowel or square section wood will be quite strong enough for this simple rack

and if you make it reasonably well and strongly it will last you for the production of hundreds of candles.

Across the fixed bars you need two movable bars that actually support the moulds. The movable bars need to be clipped firmly to the fixed ones with clothes pins or large paper fasteners, once you have the mould in position, otherwise they may move just at the wrong moment and let your mould full of hot wax fall over. The moulds themselves are very light, and do not seem as if they would require much support, but remember that you may be pouring in about a pound or two of wax, and this can easily pull the mould off the rack unless the supports are firmly fixed. Hot wax softens the moulds and makes them more flexible, and this in itself can lead to sagging.

Some people prefer to support flexible moulds by wrapping them round firmly with several thicknesses of corrugated cardboard so as to make a bulky cylinder. If this is carefully wound it should stand up on its own without further support. The cardboard is fastened with a ring of cellulose tape or gummed tape. Holding up moulds in this way saves you the bother of making a rack, but the candles take longer to cool because of the insulating effect of the layers of cardboard, and there is always the danger of wrapping a mould too tightly and distorting it.

With the mould securely fixed by either method, melt your wax. At the start you may find it difficult to calculate just how much wax you need for a particular mould. This is something that soon comes with practice and experience, but Table II on page 86 will help you to work out quantities. If in doubt always melt up more wax than you need. It won't be wasted, and nothing spoils a candle more than the tell-tale line that shows where you ran out of wax and had to heat up more while the first batch cooled down. Heat the wax to about 180°F. (82°C.) for rubber moulds; if you have it much hotter it may damage the mould, and in any case the moulds tend to soften as the hot wax goes in. If the wax is too hot the mould can sag away from its supports.

Pour the wax into the mould fairly rapidly, and tap lightly all round the mould to remove air bubbles. Leave it until a well forms in the wax, and the upper surface starts to set solid, then poke a hole in the setting wax and pour in a little more wax to make the surface flat. You may have to do this more than once as the wax contracts in the mould. The idea is not only to make the base of the candle as flat as possible, but also to prevent the contraction of the wax from drawing the sides of the mould inwards and thus distorting the candle.

If the mould begins to sag, or shows signs of slipping from its support, lift it carefully and press it back into shape gently between your hands while it is still warm. Then leave it alone until it is *quite* cold. You may be anxious to see your production, especially if this is a new mould, but if you try to get the mould off while the wax is soft you are sure to spoil it. When the candle is really cold, rub the outside of the mould with soap and water, or washing-up liquid and water, and carefully peel it back from the candle, taking extra care to release the wick without pulling it too hard. Wash and dry the mould, roll it back to its original shape, and put it away somewhere safe from heat and direct sunlight.

The candle surface may contain little depressions from air bubbles. This is probably due to having the wax at too low a temperature, or not tapping the mould thoroughly enough to detach the air bubbles after you poured the wax in. If the surface is too bad, remelt the candle and start again. You won't have lost anything except a little of your time. If the candle is just a little rough in places, rub it carefully between your hands, or with a soft piece of cloth (a lint-free polishing duster is ideal, then you do not run the risk of rubbing little flecks of fluff into the wax surface). You will find that you can soon bring up a fine polish on the surface of your candle, especially if you have included a little beeswax in the mix.

Once you know how to get a good impression from your mould, you can experiment. See how the shape looks in different coloured waxes. Some moulds seem suited for light colours, pastels, and white candles, while others look better in dark rich colours. If you have one of the designs with a lot of fine detail in relief, such as a floral pattern shown in Plate 3, or the popular medieval 'stele' design, you can get a very attractive effect by putting gold or light-coloured highlights on the raised parts of the design, after making the candle in dark-coloured wax. An easy way to do this with a cylindrical candle is to brush out gold lacquer paint or gold water-proof ink on a flat surface, such as a piece of flat plastic or a glazed tray, and then simply roll the candle lightly over the paint. The high points pick up highlights, and you can decorate several candles with one spread of paint. Don't overdo the amount of colour, otherwise the pigment will get into the wax as the candle burns and may clog the wick. If you want to be really precise, or your candle is an awkward shape, you can paint the highlights on with a small camel-hair artists' brush.

Commercial *silicone rubber* moulds are treated similarly to rubber moulds. They are more expensive, but they give better detail in intricate designs, and stand up to more wear. The main point to watch when working with this type of mould is that it needs to be removed from the candle with even more care than a rubber mould, as silicone rubber tends to be tougher than the candle itself and a careless tug can spoil the detail in the wax.

Metal moulds

Metal moulds are sold for making shapes that have less fine detail than those made in rubber or silicone rubber, and are best for shapes with precise sharp edges and corners. If you want ultra-modern designs with hard edges, search out good metal moulds. As metal is rigid, and also a good conductor of heat, the technique for casting is slightly different from that used for flexible moulds.

Make sure that the inside of the mould is completely clean and dry. Wax your wick, just as if you were preparing it for a rubber mould, and thread it through the hole in the top of the mould, fixing it with mould seal. You can pull it tight by tying the other end to a piece of stick or plastic rod, rolling up the wick, and resting the stick across the open end of the mould.

Work out how much wax you need to fill the mould (Table II will help you with this) and melt the wax, raising the temperature to 190°F. (88°C.). Pour it into the mould, and tap the outside of the mould lightly to get rid of air bubbles. Then lower the mould carefully into a bath of cold water – a large kitchen basin or a plastic bucket of cold water will do very well for this. Try to arrange the amount of water so that the level outside the mould is the same as the level of wax inside. This will make sure that the wax cools evenly. Don't, whatever you do, have the level of water so high that it runs over into the mould.

You may find at this stage that you need a weight to hold down the mould. Wax is lighter than water, and a large candle, even in a metal mould, may have a tendency to float and tip over. A kitchen weight, or a saucer, or some similar heavy object will help to keep the mould down in the cooling water.

Let the candle cool until a well forms round the wick by contraction of the wax, then break up the surface of the wax and carefully add more hot wax to fill up the depression.

You will find with metal moulds that this stage requires more care than with flexible moulds. This is because metal moulds are rigid, and cannot be peeled back from the finished candle. You are depending on the contraction of the wax to make sure that the candle comes out of the mould satisfactorily. If you put too much extra wax on top of the cooling candle, you will make a wedge that prevents the candle from sliding out of the mould (see Figure 13).

Once you have a flat base to the candle, leave it alone to cool, then slide it out of the mould. If it sticks, try dipping the whole mould into hot water *very briefly*, but this is really an emergency measure, as it tends to spoil the surface of the candle. If you have avoided forming a 'wedge' when topping-up the wax, and your wax mixture is properly formulated, you should have no difficulties.

Trim the wick, and level the base with a sharp knife. You will find that candles made in metal moulds with water cooling need very little polishing as they have a

FIG. 13 Using metal moulds. When you fill the mould (1) the wax begins to contract from the top and from the sides (2 – shown exaggerated). You should aim just to fill the dip at the top with wax (3). If you overfill the wax runs down the sides of the contracted candle and makes a wedge that causes difficulties in removing the candle (4).

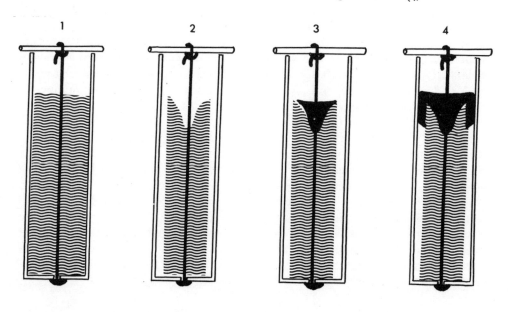

natural glossy surface. If you cool slowly, in the air, the finish will be more mat. This can be useful if you want to paint the candle afterwards.

Don't put the mould into water before you pour in the wax – this gives you a very irregular surface, and your candle may be covered with unsightly scales which flake off.

Variations on metal-moulded candles

Candles made in metal moulds have a precision and sharpness that is completely different from that of candles made in flexible moulds or by hand. This effect may please you at first, but after a time you will probably begin to think that the candles lack character, and have a monotony that is inseparable from 'machine-made' products. Fortunately, once you possess one or two metal moulds, you can ring the changes on your products in a number of ways. Most of these ideas can also be used for other moulds as well as metal, but they are particularly suitable for livening up the square-cut, plain candle that results from most metal moulds.

Chunky candles

This variation is a good way of using up odds and ends of coloured wax left over from other candle-making operations, or you can make up coloured pieces specially. You need strongly coloured wax in a variety of colours, and white or pale-coloured wax as background.

Make your coloured waxes into cubes or oblongs about $\frac{1}{2}$ in. to 1 in. per side. You can easily do this by melting the wax and pouring it into small box lids or clean dry empty food cans, letting it set right through, and then cutting up the wax into chunks with a sharp knife.

Place these chunks into a metal mould haphazardly, mixing the colours as you think best, and not forgetting to put the wick into position before you start tossing in the chunks. Then melt some light-coloured wax to about 200°F. (93°C.) and pour this over the chunks, tapping the mould to prevent air bubbles being trapped in the mould between the chunks. Top up with melted wax in the usual way as it contracts.

Don't use pieces less than about $\frac{1}{2}$ in. in any direction, or you will find that they melt into the background wax and become no more than a series of coloured smears, like a half-melted tutti-frutti ice cream. You can use irregular-shaped pieces of wax for your chunks, and according to your taste have a riot of contrasting colours or just a few selected shades.

If you are mixing your own waxes, there are several variations on this method that may give you interesting results. If, for example, you make the coloured chunks from pure stearin coloured with dyes, or from a mixture of stearin and hard micro-crystalline wax, they will not melt so easily when you pour in the background wax, and the colours will stand out brighter and more 'hard-edged'. If for the background colour you use pure hard paraffin wax (melting-point 135–140°F., 57–60°C.) the background will be slightly more transparent than if you add stearin to the wax, and therefore show up the chunks better.

Another effect which is quite distinctive is obtained by making a chunky candle and then carving away the background colour from the outside with a sharp knife, leaving the coloured chunks standing out as irregular projections, like a lump of multicoloured rock or a cluster of gem-stones.

Multilayered candles

Candles in stripes, layers and patches are very popular among candlemakers, and make a pleasant change from the conventional moulded candle. They can be made in almost any type of mould, but you will find that a fairly plain shape, like most metal moulds, will give the best results. Stripes and patches of contrasting colours in an elaborately detailed moulding tend to look fussy and overdone.

The important matter to master in making any multilayered candle is the temperature control. If your waxes are too hot and soft when you pour one on another, the layers will run together and you will just end up with a mess. If the waxes are too cold or hard, the layers will not stick together properly and you will find that the candles crack apart at the joins between the colours.

The best way to make these candles is to have all your colours ready for use at the right temperature, which is ideally about 180°F. (82°C.). If you have made up a thermostatically controlled water-bath as described in Chapter 2 this will be easy. Otherwise, put your waxes in clean dry food cans, or mugs. Whichever you use, put these in a large saucepan of water, and try to keep the temperature around 180°F. by adjusting the heat carefully.

To make your candle, pour in the first layer of wax at 180°F. and let it cool until the surface is just rubbery, then pour the next layer. You will soon get the 'feel' of this, and if you pour each layer carefully, you should have no trouble with disturbance of the previous colour layer.

When you have filled the mould, let the whole candle cool in water, and slide it out in the normal way. Trim the wick and level the base.

There is no reason why the layers need be horizontal and parallel. If you tilt the mould, you can have layers at any angle, and some very bizarre results can be obtained by tilting the mould at different angles for each colour (see Plate 4). Try to find something to hold the mould at the right angle each time – I use a laboratory stand and clamp, but you can support one side of the mould on a block of wood or a book to steady it as you pour (see Figure 14).

If you want diffused colours, instead of sharp edges between them, you can use a

FIG. 14 Tilting metal moulds. Your layered candles do not have to have horizontal stripes only: you can tilt the mould by resting it on a block of wood or a book as in the left-hand picture, and fill it up with layers of wax set at different angles.

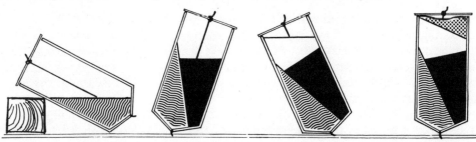

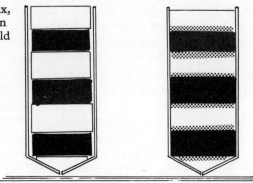

FIG. 15 Rough layer candles. Slabs of wax, roughly the size of the mould, are piled on one another (left-hand sketch). The mould is then put in hot water until they run together (right-hand sketch).

modification of the 'chunky' system. Take a suitable mould, and cut up pieces of coloured wax that nearly fill it from side to side. Place these one on another so that you have a kind of very rough multilayered candle (see Figure 15). Then immerse the mould in hot water and leave it until you can see that the wax pieces are melting. At this point take the mould out of the hot water and put it into cooling water. When it sets and is removed from the mould you will find that the layers are quite clearly defined, but instead of sharp contrasting edges they have a diffused layer in between each pair of colours, blue and yellow having made green, and so on. The depth of the diffused zone will vary according to the amount of time that the mould was left in hot water.

A charming effect of this kind can be obtained if you start off with layers of bright red, yellow, and violet-blue, or preferably red, yellow, indigo blue, and red again. If these are allowed to diffuse together a rainbow or spectrum effect can be obtained. It takes a little practice, but the effect is well worthwhile.

Ice candles
This is a technique for making mysterious and fascinating holes and caverns in the conventional-shaped candle.

You need a wick which is already heavily waxed. You can do this yourself by dipping, or use a ready-made small candle. If you dip a candle yourself, leave enough of the wick to thread through the hole of a metal mould or if you are using a ready-made commercial candle, melt off some of the wax at the top to give you enough wick to thread through.

With the wick in position, place the mould in the freezer of your refrigerator, or as near as you can get to it. While it is chilling, melt your wax and keep it at 190°F. (88°C.). Crush some ice cubes so that you have irregular-shaped pieces of ice, and drop the crushed ice into the chilled mould. Most of the ice will stick round the sides of the mould.

Pour the wax into the mould quickly, and place the mould immediately in cooling water. When it is quite cold, turn out your candle. You will find that the ice has melted, leaving holes all round the outside of the candle and a general effect like some strange geological feature.

It is necessary to use the heavily waxed wick because otherwise water could get

47

into the threads of the wick and prevent proper burning of the finished candle. Its use also ensures that the centre of the candle is solid – an 'ice-hole' round the wick could lead to very irregular burning.

Stratified candles

Just as you can make candles with strata of different colours by successive dipping (see p. 38), you can reverse the process and make them in metal moulds.

Have all your coloured waxes ready at 180°F. (82°C.). You will need enough of each colour to fill the mould melted, although you will not be using all this material finally. Choose the colour you want for the outside of the candle, pour this into the mould until it is full, and immediately put the mould into the cooling bath. As soon as the wax on the outside begins to set, pour the remainder of the wax back into your can or boiler, and leave a thin layer adhering to the mould. Then carefully pour the next layer, repeating the procedure, then the next, and so on, until the mould is full. When the candle is turned out of the mould you can carve back holes in the sides to show the various colours underneath, just as with a dipped stratified candle.

It is worth saying here that with every type of multicoloured candle you are sure to have failures from time to time. Remember that if you remelt the wax from such candles all the colours will mix, and usually the result is a rather dull brown wax. Keep this for there are many occasions when a fairly drab material can be used successfully to contrast with brighter shades, and it also looks very well when used for the 'antique' type of candle, like the medieval one in Plate 3. A touch of gold paint on such a candle works wonders, and the brown wax can be lightened, if necessary, with plain white wax to make a parchment or ivory colour.

PLASTER MOULDING

Ready-made moulds are very useful, but the range is limited, and you will probably want to express your own ideas in candle making and make your own moulds. There are several methods of doing this, but plaster moulding is one of the most useful and easy to start on.

Plaster of Paris is made from the mineral gypsum, a hard white material, by drying out some of the water that is chemically bound to the gypsum, calcium sulphate. When water is added to plaster it gets hot, the water recombines with the calcium sulphate, and gypsum is formed again, but this takes a few minutes to happen. During this time the mixture of plaster and water can be used to take an impression of any solid shape, or it can be poured into a mould, and when it sets to gypsum it will hold that shape. Plaster expands slightly as it sets, and this makes it a good medium for casting detailed objects. The expansion forces the plaster into every little depression and detail on the surface, or, in a mould, the plaster expands to fill the mould tightly and thus takes a very exact impression.

Plaster of Paris can be bought from artists' suppliers and craft stores and it should not be confused with the wall plaster used by builders and decorators, which is almost useless for casting and craft work. Wall plaster takes several hours to set, and it is usually so full of grit and sand that it can never take a good impression of fine detail.

48

PLATE 3 Candles from rubber moulds. The two at the front are from silicone rubber moulds.

PLATE 4   A chunky candle (centre) and various multilayered candles.

As an example of the technique of plaster mould casting, a good project is a wax apple.

You will need a large firm apple with a good shape and free of insect bites or flaws. The colour and appearance, of course, do not matter at all; it is only the shape that we want to copy. Most apples have a natural layer of wax on the surface, but if you want to be quite sure of getting your apple out of the mould without damage, you can rub it over with a clean tissue dipped in salad oil or cooking fat, so as to leave the surface slightly greasy. You also need a cardboard or plastic box at least an inch larger all round than the apple: if your apple is 3 ins. in diameter, you need a box at least 5 ins. square and deep. It can be larger than this, but then you will need more plaster. The plastic boxes sold for storing food in refrigerators are very suitable, especially if they are the type that taper slightly from top to bottom.

Mix plaster and water to a smooth cream, not too thin but pourable, and pour this into the box until it fills about a third of the space. The plaster will now have air bubbles in it. Shake the box gently from side to side to get rid of as much air as possible, then, as the plaster begins to harden, push the apple into it until it is half immersed. Push the apple in sideways, so that the stalk and the small depression for the calyx at the other end give you a 'half-way mark'. As you push, move the apple very slightly from side to side as this helps to ensure that air bubbles are not trapped under the plaster. Then, when you can feel the hardening plaster is able to support the apple by itself, let go and leave the plaster to set thoroughly.

After an hour or two the plaster should be quite hard. Carefully remove the apple and check that you have a good impression in the plaster.

This gives you half a mould. Now you need the other half, but before you cast it there are two things to do. First, you need some way of ensuring that the two halves of the mould always come together in the same way. The simplest way of doing this is to drill two holes about $\frac{1}{4}$ in. deep in the plaster of the first part of the mould. Plaster is easy to cut into – you can make the holes with a knife blade or by drilling a small conical hole with a countersink bit in a hand-drill. Make the holes about half-way between the 'apple' shape and the edge of the plaster. When you pour plaster on to make the second half of the mould, it will flow into these depressions and form corresponding projections, so that the two halves of the mould can always be fitted together exactly by plugging the projections into the holes.

The second thing to do is to treat the surface of the first half of the mould with some material that will stop the fresh plaster sticking to it, otherwise you will have an apple permanently embedded in a solid block of plaster! There are many materials that will prevent this sticking. Soap is the traditional one, but some of the silicone release agents now available are better. If you wish to use soap, or cannot find the silicone material, ask a chemist or drug store for some soft soap, and make up a solution of equal parts of soft soap and alcohol (ordinary methylated spirit). You can paint this on the plaster with a paintbrush. Most craft suppliers who deal with candlemakers' wants will have a silicone release fluid, however.

When you have the first half of the mould prepared in this way, place the apple back exactly in position and pour plaster over it until it is entirely covered by at least 1 in. of plaster all over. Shake the mould gently to release air bubbles, as before, and leave it to set. After an hour or two you should be able to remove the

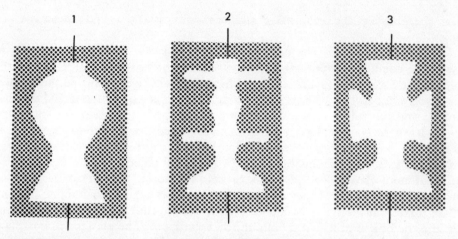

FIG. 16 Plaster moulds. Shapes like (1) are easy to cast. With (2) there may be some difficulty in removing the original and the candles from the mould, while shapes like (3) with undercutting are impossible to cast because you would have to break the mould to get the original out.

mould by shaking it out of the plastic box, separate the two halves, and rescue the apple.

Paint the second half of the mould with silicone mould release agent or soft soap solution. This is partly to stop it from sticking to the other half of the plaster, but mainly to ensure that the candles that you cast will come away easily from the mould. Then put both halves of the mould away to dry. This stage is very important if you want to make good-looking candles from plaster moulds. Damp plaster gives very poor results, because steam from the plaster will spoil the surface of the wax. Leave your moulds on a radiator or in a hot cupboard for at least three days before you attempt to use them.

All that remains now is to carve a small groove in each half at the stalk end of the apple, to hold the wick, and a larger hole at the base end to allow you to pour in the wax. You can easily do this with a knife. To fasten the wick, fix it across the middle of one half of the mould, take it through the grooves that you have made, and then tie it on the outside of the mould. Put the two halves of the mould together, tie them round with string so that they cannot separate, and make sure that the wick is not loose at the stalk end (if necessary seal the hole with mould seal).

Plaster moulds tend to chill wax, so I prefer to warm the whole mould through before casting. If you put the assembled mould in a warm oven for half an hour before use, this should warm it through quite satisfactorily. Place the warm mould on a sheet of paper, melt your wax to about 200°F. (93°C.), and pour it carefully through the hole in the base of the mould, tapping the mould down on the table from time to time to make sure that air bubbles are escaping. Fill right up until no more wax will go in – the contraction in this case will give you a lifelike base to the apple. Leave the mould to cool, remembering that plaster cools slowly and therefore you will have to wait longer than with a metal mould. Then untie the string round the mould and gently prise the two halves apart (you can put a knife

50

blade in between the halves, being careful not to stab the wax inside). Trim the wick and polish the 'apple' with a soft cloth.

A very realistic variation on this candle can be obtained if you cast the apple in green or yellowish wax, with red stripes or blush marks just as in some varieties of apple. All you need to do is to melt some red wax when the moulds are still separate, and run thin streams of wax over the inside surfaces in stripes or patches according to the effect you want. This will look very crude at this stage, but when you put the mould halves together and pour in the hot green or yellow wax the red will diffuse into quite natural-looking details on the surface of the apple.

Similar methods can be used for any simple shape. Be careful not to choose objects to cast that have 'undercut' portions (see Figure 16), otherwise you will never get them out of the plaster mould except by breaking it.

The Hand of Glory

If you have a taste for the macabre, you may like to make an up-to-date version of a device used in medieval black magic, the *Maindegloire* or Hand of Glory.

In the days when the bodies of hanged criminals were hung in chains on gibbets (a barbarous custom that persisted up to as late as 1832 in England) it was believed that a hand cut off from the body had strange magical powers. It was made into a grotesque torch or candle by soaking it in human fat, usually from a dead child. Bodies hung on gibbets were quite often covered with pitch or tar to preserve them – they were intended as dreadful warnings that crime does not pay – so this must have added further fuel. This object was known as a *Maindegloire* or Hand of Glory, and it was popularly believed in the sixteenth and seventeenth centuries that if thieves made themselves such a candle and lighted it in front of a house, all the locks and bars on the doors would burst apart as the Hand approached, and the inhabitants of the house would be thrown into a deep sleep so that they could not interfere with the burglars.

Apart from this macabre story, a hand-shaped candle is a striking, if not very pleasant, decoration. You can cast a small glass or china hand, or you can do the job properly and make a plaster mould from your own hand.

First find a cardboard box rather bigger than your hand with the fingers slightly spread, and about $2\frac{1}{2}$–3 ins. deep. If you cannot find a suitable box, you can easily make one out of card folded and glued into shape. In one end, cut a U-shaped hollow to accommodate your wrist, so that you can put your hand in the box comfortably with about $\frac{1}{2}$–1 in. of wrist inside – this will form the base of the candle.

Next grease your hand to make sure it releases from the plaster easily. Petroleum jelly or any hand cream will do for this. The left hand is traditional for the Hand of Glory, which is convenient for most people because they can then use their right hands for pouring the plaster. If, like me, you are left-handed, you will have to decide whether to be traditional or comfortable.

Mix enough plaster almost to fill the box, and place your hand in position, palm downwards, with the fingers slightly apart. Remember that when your candle is cast the fingers will be lighted, and if they are too splayed out the wax will drip badly from the little finger and thumb. Try to keep your fingers and thumb as nearly parallel as possible.

51

Pour the plaster into the box until it comes about half-way up your hand and fingers. Keep your wrist pressed down firmly in its hollow so that plaster cannot leak out of the end of the box. Then *keep still* until the plaster has set. You will have to be very patient about this, and this is one good reason for casting your own hand, rather than asking someone else to 'model' for you. At least you have the thought that a single twitch at the wrong time will spoil *your* casting.

You will know when the plaster is nearly set because of the heat produced as the water reacts to form gypsum. Press down very cautiously with one of your fingers, and when you feel that the plaster is hard, carefully ease your hand out of the mould. You should have a perfect impression with the lines and fingerprints complete.

Drill two or three hollows in the plaster outside the hand shape, to make locating points for the two halves of the mould when it is complete, and coat the mould with soap or mould release compound as with other plaster moulds. Then build up the cardboard surround to take the second half of the mould. This is easily done by cutting a strip of cardboard about 3 ins. wide and sticking it to three sides of the box, so that the box is now 2–2½ ins. deeper. Leave the side with the hollow for the wrist open for the moment.

Now you will have to put your hand back in the mould. This means that you will not be able to move from the spot very easily, so have all the things you need for the second half of the mould ready to hand: plaster, water, and a mixing vessel are obvious, but also have gummed tape cut into short lengths of 3–4 ins. and some Plasticine or modelling clay.

With your hand in position in the lower half of the mould, build up the fourth side of the box round your wrist with pieces of gummed tape, and finish the sealing off with Plasticine. Now mix the plaster and water, and pour this over your hand so as to fill the upper half of the box. Again wait until the plaster gets hot and sets. Leave it as long as your patience will stand, and then cut through the cardboard at the join, flex your fingers gently, and the two halves of the mould should come apart easily. Put them aside to dry thoroughly, after painting the top half with silicone release agent or soap.

Now you need to fit the wicks, along each finger and the thumb. Figure 17 shows the details of this. Cut a groove with a knife at the end of each 'finger' on the mould, running the groove out to the edge of the mould. Select five pieces of wick long enough to run the full length of the mould from end to end, and tie a small piece of stick, a curtain ring, or some similar object to each one. Lay each length of wick in its appropriate groove with the sticks or rings to stop them pulling right through, and draw the other ends of the wicks through the wrist hole of the mould. Fasten these ends to a larger piece of stick that can be used to tighten them up.

If you want long sinister fingernails on the candle, you can carve these out of the upper half of the mould by gouging out plaster with a knife at the end of each 'fingernail'. Then assemble the mould, make sure the wicks are in position, tie the two halves of the mould together securely, and warm it ready for pouring. Heat the wax to about 200°F. (93°C.). There is quite a choice of appropriate colours. Black looks sinister and occult, but a pale greenish white has a definite graveyard look about it. If your plaster casting has been successful, you should have every line

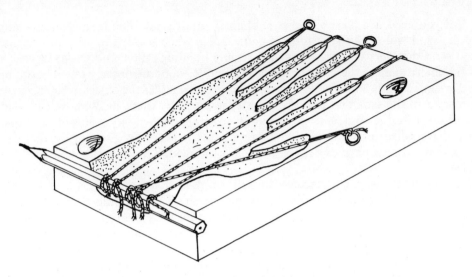

FIG. 17 How to assemble the wicks for the 'Hand of Glory'. A pencil or stick can be used to tighten them at the wrist end, while curtain rings or similar fastenings are used at each finger end. Note the depressions carved out to ensure that the two halves of the mould fit together in the same way every time.

and detail of your hand present in the wax copy, and this in itself is creepy, especially when you light the candle and the 'fingers' begin to burn away.

Just one piece of practical advice. If you have fine hair on the back of your hands, shave or clip it off before you make the upper half of the mould. Otherwise the plaster will take it off for you, very painfully, when you try to get your hand out of the mould!

You can make a hand moulded in a rubber glove, but this is far less realistic.

Other plaster moulds
There is really no limit to the number of things that you can cast in plaster and use to make successful candles. Fruit and vegetables, like the apple, are easy to copy and make very effective decorations. Small figures and statuettes (as long as they have no undercut parts), vases and ornaments and most other small solid objects can be cast. Just remember to lubricate them well before you pour plaster over them. Miniature wine and liqueur bottles are easy to cast, and if you can get or draw miniature labels to match, can be turned into unusual decorative candles.

If you have any skill in modelling, you can make your own candle shapes in Plasticine or clay, cast these in plaster, and use the plaster moulds to produce candles. Try modelling caricatures of your friends or of people in the news, and turn these into candles for gifts.

SAND-CAST CANDLES
Casting candles in sand is an adaptation of the standard engineers' method of making copies of machine parts, and so on. However, in the case of candle wax, you will find that the sand becomes an integral part of the finished candle, not just a moulding medium.

All you need is a plastic bucket of slightly moist sand. The texture and colour of the sand will form the outside of your candle when it is made, so choose a fine soft sand that does not look dirty, as so many building sands tend to do. Choose a solid object to make the basic shape of the candle – a bottle or jar, a small basin, or some similar thing – and press this firmly into the sand. If the object is large, scoop out some of the sand first to make it easier to push the shape in. Remove the solid carefully from the sand, and smooth away any roughness or any grains of sand that may have fallen into the hole. You can adapt the shape by pressing further depressions with the bowl of a spoon or a piece of wood. This hole is now to be filled with wax.

Obviously the wax will percolate into the sand, so that more or less sand is stuck to the outer surface of the candle. The amount that sticks, and thus the thickness of the sand layer, depends on two factors – the moisture in the sand and the temperature of the wax. If you have wet sand, or the temperature of the wax is below 200°F. (93°C.), not much sand will be picked up and you will just have a thin coating that can, if you wish, be carved off altogether. If the sand is almost dry – just moist enough to hold its shape – and the wax is really hot (above 212°F., 100°C.), a thick layer of sand will be stuck to the candle. Most people who make sand-cast candles want the texture of sand on the outside (after all, there are better ways of making a plain candle than casting it in sand and then having to clean off the sand again).

Making sand-covered candles immediately poses a problem. It is necessary to use wax at higher temperatures than the boiling-point of water, and therefore you cannot use your double boiler or water-bath. Heating wax directly always involves a serious risk of fire, so before you embark on sand-cast candles READ THE FIRE PRECAUTIONS ON PAGE 31. In particular, always remember to turn the stove off before removing wax from the heat, and if the wax should catch fire, *do not use water* to put it out for this will just spread the fire and may result in you being splashed with hot wax. Always smother a wax fire. If you are working with a saucepan, put the saucepan lid on.

The highest temperature to which it is safe to heat wax is about 350°F. (177°C.), but this is quite enough to give a thick coating of sand on a candle. About 320°F. (160°C.) is probably the best temperature at which to work. Carefully pour the wax into the sand mould, taking care not to pour it on the edges of the mould where it could disturb the sand. You will find that it takes more wax than you would expect because of the amount that is absorbed by the sand.

When the mould is full and the surface is becoming rubbery, push a small hole through the centre with a knitting-needle or similar thin metal rod for the wick. Lead-stiffened wick is very good for this purpose. Choose a smaller size of wick than the size of the candle suggests. For example, if your mould is 3 ins. in diameter use a wick for a 2-in. candle. This will ensure that the candle burns hollow and ultimately the flame will burn in a kind of sandy pit.

As the candle cools, the wax will contract and form a central depression. Top this up with molten wax and cool as quickly as possible by blowing or using a fan. This will produce a shiny top. Finally, when the candle is quite cold, dig it carefully out of the sand, brush off loose sand, and make sure that it is reasonably symmetrical.

54

The candle in this form will seem very rough and clumsy. There are several ways in which it can be improved. You can carve it back to the original shape with a sharp knife, or you can carve right through the sand in places to make 'windows' with wax showing. When the candle flame burns down a little, these windows will show through as lighted areas in the sand. You can carve simple holes, or complicated shapes and letters. If there is any loose sand left on the surface, roll the candle quickly in melted wax, or dip it in melted wax if the shape is too complicated for rolling.

HOME-MADE RUBBER MOULDS

There are quite a number of shapes that do not lend themselves to casting in plaster, because of undercutting or deep cavities in the design, and flexible moulds would obviously be better than plaster for these. Also, flexible moulds can be made in one piece, very often, while plaster moulds almost invariably have to be made in two halves fitting together.

Fortunately it is quite easy to use the special type of synthetic rubber employed for making flexible moulds, and almost any solid shape can be copied in this way. The same flexible moulding material is used for a number of crafts and industries. It can be turned into moulds for plaster or polystyrene casting resin as well as for candle wax, and it is available from craft suppliers and also from many suppliers of plastics raw materials.

The simplest type of rubber to use is the re-meltable kind. This material can be melted down after it has been used for a mould and turned into some other shape. This is particularly useful for the beginner. Not only can you re-use your moulds when you are tired of them, but you need not worry about wasting material if your moulds do not turn out exactly right first time. Like wax, you can melt up the rubber and start again. Most suppliers sell three grades of re-meltable rubber – very flexible (useful for very complicated shapes), medium flexible, and hard. Often these are colour-coded. Quite a lot of moulding rubber is sold in green for very flexible, red for medium, and yellow for hard.

The medium type is the best one to start on. Very flexible rubber can take any shape, but it is so floppy that it is difficult to make the moulds keep their shape when you pour the wax. The hard variety makes splendidly firm moulds, but it is so stiff that it is difficult to remove from the finished candles without damaging them.

Most varieties of the re-meltable rubber soften at about 250°F. (121°C.) and melt enough for pouring at about 280°F. (138°C.), so they will stand up to the heat of hot wax quite easily. On the other hand, you cannot melt them in your double boiler or water-bath. Some companies supplying the rubber can also supply a special double melting vessel that is filled with oil and if you intend to make many moulds this is a good investment. Otherwise you will have to use an old saucepan and keep a careful check on the temperature with your thermometer. Have a fairly stout piece of wood for stirring the rubber as this will keep it from burning on the bottom of the saucepan. Most re-meltable rubber smells rather unpleasant as it is melting, so if you can, try to do this part of the work near an open window or in a room where there is a good extractor fan.

Suppose you want to make a candle in the shape of a cut-glass flower vase. You

55

have a little vase of the right type, and you need to make a flexible mould from it.

Put about $\frac{1}{2}$ lb. of the rubber in your melting pot or saucepan, and gently heat it up until the temperature is around 250°F. (121°C.), stirring all the time as it begins to soften. Carry on heating until the temperature is over 275°F. (135°C.). The rubber should now be melting to a thick sticky liquid. Keep it stirred steadily as it melts, until all the lumps have dispersed. Try to hold the temperature between 275° and 280°F. (135–138°C.) (although you may have to alter these temperatures according to the exact grade of rubber that you have. The temperatures given are those for the most widely distributed types).

Now pick up your little vase by the neck and roll its lower half in the rubber, keeping it moving. Lift it out, still rotating it slowly, and it should be covered with an even layer of rubber. *Do not touch this.* It will be a lot hotter than it looks, and the rubber has a nasty habit of sticking to the skin, thus making any burn far worse. Having covered the base of the vase thoroughly, stand it on a sheet or clean paper on a flat heat-proof surface and carefully pour the melted rubber over it, trying to get an even coating all over. Some of the rubber will run right down on to the paper, but do not worry about this. It can be picked up when it is cold, and used again. When the vase is covered, leave it to cool completely, then peel it off the paper. Cut round fairly close to the vase with scissors to remove the excess rubber that ran down on to the paper, and carefully peel back the rubber mould from the vase. You should have an exact impression.

If there are too many air bubbles in the surface of the mould, or a hole that you did not notice when you poured the rubber, you may decide to try again. All you have to do is to remelt the stock rubber and put the unsatisfactory mould back with the rest. Try pouring at a slightly higher temperature for your next attempt. This will make it easier for air bubbles to escape and for the rubber to flow right over the surface of the vase.

Moulds made in this way can be used in exactly the same way as commercial rubber moulds. With practice you will even be able to make a ring of rubber round the base of each mould to act as a stiffener when you hang it up for pouring the wax. Any unwanted parts of the rubber can be peeled away and cut off with scissors or a knife. Put all these left-overs in your stock of rubber for making other moulds.

You will find that the rubber will stand up to about twelve to fifteen meltings, depending how carefully you heat it. After a time it begins to darken, as small portions tend to overheat and burn, and when it gets too dark it is best to throw it away. The material is not very expensive.

You can make moulds in this way from any object that can stand the temperature of 280°F. (138°C.) – glass, china, wood, most plastics (but be careful with these), plaster, metal – the list is endless. Don't try to take a mould from a painted object unless you are not worried about the state of the paint – the hot rubber tends to blister it.

A particularly suitable project for candle making with home-made rubber moulds is a chess set. The repetitions needed for two each of the kings and queens, four bishops, four knights, four castles, and sixteen pawns make full use of the moulds, so you can feel that the trouble of making them is well worthwhile. Find an attractive set of pieces in wood, plastic, or ivory, and make careful moulds of one each of the king, queen, bishop, knight, castle, and pawn. Then fit these moulds with wicks in the usual way, and go on to cast the full set of pieces, in contrasting colours. Red and white or red and ivory always look attractive for chessmen.

For high precision work, and models with a lot of fine detail, silicone rubber makes better moulds than the ordinary re-meltable kind. It is handled in exactly the same way – although according to the grade you obtain it may have to be melted at a higher temperature – but it is as well to remember that it is more expensive, and cannot be re-melted and used again, so keep silicone rubber for your show-pieces. The moulds are very hard wearing. P.S. Bennett, who made the traditional English fireman's helmet in Plate 6, has produced thousands of candles to sell for charity, using silicone rubber-type moulds.

IMPROVISED MOULDS
Because candles have so much intrinsic attraction due to their colours and textures, there is an enormous scope for variations in the shapes, from the simplest geometrical forms to the most complicated and floral types. Often very striking candles can be made in moulds formed from the humblest of raw materials. Ordinary plastic packs, such as are sold for yogurt and other foods, plastic detergent containers, shampoo packages, and similar household articles can all be pressed into service. Look around the kitchen and bathroom and see how many moulds you can find.

If they are thin plastic, it is usually easy to pierce them in the right place to take the wick for the candle, but if you cannot make a hole easily, you can always put the wick in after moulding the candle. Either drill a hole with an ordinary hand-drill and a fine bit, or push a hot knitting-needle down the centre of the candle. You can then put the wick in – lead-stiffened wick is ideal for this purpose – and pour a little wax into the centre of the candle to fill up any space between the wick and the body of the candle. If you are using the soft flexible polythene type of bottle, which is employed for most of the cheap packs for detergents, etc., make sure that you do not pour your wax at too high a temperature. Polythene is very similar to wax in its properties, including having a fairly low melting-point, so keep your wax temperature down to about 180°F. (82°C.).

If you have plastic bottles with screw necks, such as are used for shampoo and similar products, you will find that a razor-blade or craftworkers' knife will easily take off the neck, leaving you a useful cylinder or other shape to use as a mould.

An ordinary rubber ball, such as a discarded tennis ball, makes a good mould. Cut through the ball carefully along a half-way mark, but don't quite divide it into two halves. Leave a small 'hinge' of rubber to help keep it closed when you are moulding. Pierce a hole for the wick to go through, in the middle of one half of the ball, and cut a hole about half an inch in diameter in the opposite half to pour in the wax.

It is best to rub the inside of the ball with silicone release agent, but you will usually find that even without this the wax will come away from the rubber quite easily.

Fit the wick in the usual way, close the ball up and keep it shut by putting rubber-bands round the middle, then pour your wax. You should be able to get a perfect sphere if you are careful not to squeeze the ball too tightly when fastening it shut.

FIG. 18 A bunch of grapes candle. The grapes are cast in refrigerator ice moulds and stuck round a wick.

Another household mould that can be pressed into service is the ordinary refrigerator ice tray. The type with cubes can be used to make 'bricks' for building up geometrical shapes (you will need to put the wick in last, using the hot needle technique and lead-stiffened wick), while the circular type has been used very effectively to make wax 'grapes' in pale green or dark purple, which are then stuck to a wick that forms the stalk for a bunch of grapes. A drop or two of hot wax can be placed on each 'grape' to stick it to the wick (see Figure 18).

Household materials with embossed or indented patterns can be used to make moulds that will leave their patterns on the finished candles. For example, if you can find a piece of embossed wallpaper or vinyl wall covering with an attractive pattern (not too large in scale), you can roll a length of this into a cylinder or cone and stick it with wallpaper paste or other adhesive. This will then make candles with an attractive design apparently carved into them (see Figure 19).

If you make the cone shape, you can fix the wick in the normal way through the top of the cone, with the help of a little mould seal or wick seal. If you make the cylinder, it will be open at both ends and you need to rest it on a smooth surface that will not be affected by the hot wax. A smooth piece of wood is ideal, especially if you polish it with silicone mould release agent before you start your other operations. Seal the cylinder of paper or vinyl to the base with mould seal or Plasticine, and use a lead-stiffened wick standing free (see page 22). Then pour your wax.

The corrugated type of plastic roofing material will also make an interesting mould. Cut a piece of the material about 8–9 ins. long (that is, at right angles to the corrugations) and about 4 ins. wide, and roll this round into a cylinder, making sure that the corrugations fit together at the join. Fix the ends with a strong paper clip at each side, then place the cylinder on your base-board and seal the base with mould seal. You can use this in exactly the same way as the paper cylinder, with a free-standing wick made of lead-stiffened material.

This mould can be used to give rather an unusual two-colour effect. Choose your colours, say white for the main colour and blue for decoration. Fit up the mould as described, with a free-standing wick, and pour in white wax until the mould is about three-quarters full. Top up to keep the surface as nearly flat as possible. Then, before the wax has hardened properly, press in each indentation of the mould with your fingers – the material is quite flexible and the wax should move easily. Don't push in very far; all you want to do is to make a small space between each indentation in the wax and the corresponding part of the mould.

Now wait until the white wax has cooled a little more, but is still in a rubbery state, and pour on the blue wax to fill the mould. Blue wax will run down into each little space that you have pressed in, and give a series of vertical stripes round the candle, under the general upper layer of solid blue colour.

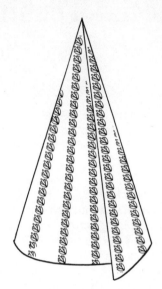

FIG. 19 Improvised mould. An attractive candle can be made by rolling a piece of embossed wallpaper or plastic into a cone, sticking it round, and using this as a mould.

Chapter 5

Special Techniques

Candlemakers have developed a number of odd ways of treating wax to get special effects, and some of these are not easy to classify as simple hand work or mould work – in fact, some of them are not easy to classify at all! Some of these methods are described in this chapter.

WHIPPED WAX

If you have some melted wax which is cooling, you will find that you can whip it up, just like egg white, with a fork, an egg-whisk, or a kitchen mixer. Once you have beaten the air into it you will find that the wax remains like meringue – light, frothy, and soft – and you can use this whipped wax to obtain some very unusual results.

Whipped wax looks different from ordinary wax. Instead of the smooth shiny surface that most candles have, those made out of whipped wax are textured, like unpolished stone. Very often you can obtain interesting effects by contrasting this textured surface with the smooth surface of ordinary wax.

Try making some whipped wax. Take some of your coloured wax and melt it in the ordinary way, then pour it into a basin and wait until the surface just begins to skin over. Now whisk it vigorously, beating in as much air as possible. You will find that it stays soft at much lower temperatures than ordinary wax, and can be poured or spooned into a mould at temperatures down to about 150°F. (66°C.) or even lower. Make up whipped wax in two or three different colours and press these down in turn into a small mould (the simple tennis ball mould mentioned in the last chapter is very suitable), not trying to get an even layered effect but a general marbling. You will need to press the material with your fingers to avoid leaving gaps, but as the wax stays soft at relatively low temperatures you will be in no danger of burning yourself.

Finally, when the mould is practically full, melt a small amount of plain wax to 160°F. (71°C.) and pour this over the whipped wax to seal the surface.

Whipped wax can be used for almost any kind of candle already described in this book. For example, alternate layers of plain wax and whipped wax add to the interest of multilayered candles, and the contrast between the mat, opaque whipped wax and the smooth translucent ordinary wax can be very effective, even if you are only using one basic colour. Just remember to pour your ordinary wax layers at a rather lower temperature than usual, so as not to spoil the effect of the whipped wax.

PLATE 5 Two sand-moulded candles, and, at the rear, a woven beeswax sheet candle.

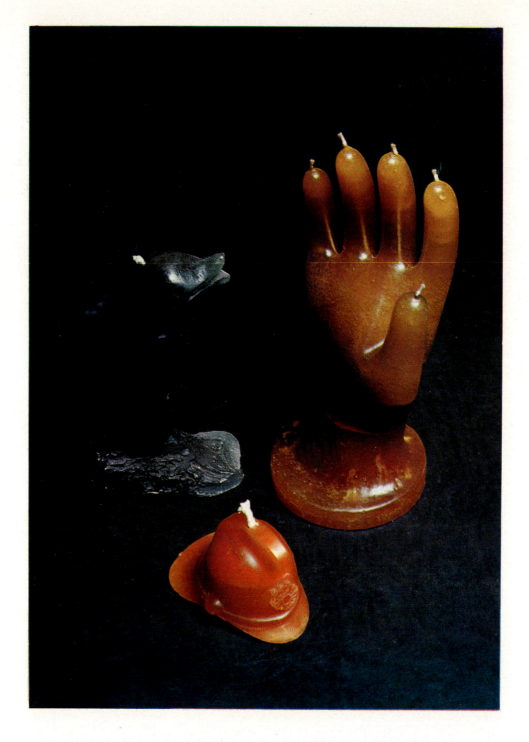

PLATE 6 Candles from home-made moulds. The hand is moulded in a rubber glove. The fireman's helmet was moulded in silicone rubber from a carving.

PLATE 7   Bottle candles. The shapes were moulded from actual miniature bottles, and labels stuck on the candles.

PLATE 8   Decorated candles. On the left, a moulded candle brushed roughly with paint. Centre, a candle with moulded decorations applied in black. Right, a candle painted with coloured stearin.

You can make up white whipped wax, which looks very bright and opaque, like snow, and use it to decorate other candles with frosting. In fact, if you are fairly quick, you can even put whipped wax into an ordinary kitchen icing cylinder, and make decorations like the traditional cake toppings.

When you are working with whipped wax, you will find that the whipping makes all the colours look lighter: wax which is quite a strong and intense colour when in the mass will only be pastel-coloured when whipped. Often pastel colours go well with the texture of whipped wax, and can be used pleasantly to contrast with the same shade, but more intense, in ordinary wax, but if you want strong colours in whipped wax you will have to mix about two to three times your normal amount of dye with the wax blend.

Another point to note is that whipped wax does not contract very much on cooling. This is reasonable, because it is not poured at such a high temperature as ordinary wax, and therefore does not have to cool so much, but it means in practice that you must be careful when using rigid moulds like metal ones. Make sure that they are thoroughly treated with mould release agent before you put whipped wax into them.

You can make an attractive variation on the 'chunky' candle using chunks in ordinary coloured wax, and a background of whipped wax. Make up some coloured chunks in the normal way, using perhaps two colours, say blue and green, and cutting the chunks fairly large, about 1 in. each way. Fit a metal mould with a wick and stretch the wick with a stick or rod as normally, then make up whipped wax in two colours that go with the chunks. In this case white and green would look well: the pale pastel green of the whipped wax will contrast well with the deeper green of the chunks.

Don't fill the mould with chunks on this occasion, or you may have difficulty in making the whipped wax surround each piece. Instead, put a layer of whipped wax in the bottom of the mould, then pile a few chunks on this at random. Cover these with whipped wax and put in more chunks, and so on until the mould is full. Press down firmly to make sure that there are no gaps, and seal the mould by pouring on a little blue or green unwhipped wax at 160°F. (71°C.) and leave the candle to cool.

When it is cool, and has come out of the mould successfully (this will depend how thoroughly you applied your mould release agent), stand it on a flat surface and carve down the sides with a sharp knife so as to reveal a clean surface of the blue and green chunks standing out against the pastel, marbled effect of the mixed white and green whipped wax. There are many variations on this technique that will repay study and experiment.

BALLOON CANDLES

This is a technique requiring a great deal of patience, care, and time, so don't embark on it if you have the odd half-hour to spare. On the other hand, the effects are very attractive and almost impossible to obtain with any other method of candle making.

The idea is to make a shell of very thin translucent wax, then pour strong colours into this and shape them into patterns. The colours then show through the wax as a kind of mysterious marbling right inside the candle. The space inside the shell is filled with plain wax and the wick is put in last. When properly made, balloon candles can be made to glow as they burn, showing off their marbling with great effect.

Because the translucency of the candle gives most of the effect in a balloon candle, they are made with *paraffin wax* alone, with no stearin added. Try to find a sample of paraffin wax that is as white as possible and has the least opacity.

As a mould, you need an ordinary rubber balloon, preferably a circular one, although you can use this technique with sausage-shaped balloons if you wish. If it is a new balloon, blow it out a little, but not enough to stretch it very much, then fill it with water, trying to get a spherical shape about 2–3 ins. in diameter. Now heat some of your paraffin wax in a vessel that will allow you to dip the balloon into the wax. Let the temperature rise to about 170°F. (77°C.) and dip the balloon into the wax, rotating it to get an even coating of wax. Lift the balloon out, still rotating it to make sure that wax spreads evenly, wait about thirty seconds and then redip for a further layer of wax, and so on for about ten layers. You will find that the balloon has to be quite dry on its outside, otherwise the wax will not adhere.

When you have a layer of wax set on the balloon, and as hard as it can be, turn the balloon upside down and let the water out. With great care you should now be able to detach the balloon from the inside of the wax, and be left with a hollow spherical shell of white wax. If you manage to make one the first time without it breaking or caving in at some point, never complain again about your luck! These shells are very fragile, but obviously the thinner they are, the more the colours will show through the wax layer.

If you are wise, make two or three more shells even after you have had one success. There are other hazards ahead.

Now you need some strong colours dissolved in stearin. Choose your colour scheme and make up the colours quite strongly in about a tablespoonful of stearin for each shade. You can melt the stearin by using a number of cups or small cans in a saucepan of hot water, having one for each colour.

Take about a teaspoonful of one of the colours, in the melted stearin, and pour it into the paraffin wax shell. Rotate the shell rapidly to swish the colour around, rather as if you were trying the bouquet of a glass of brandy. Don't let the hot stearin stay still on any part of the shell, or you will have a hole, and if you have a pool of stearin left after swirling it around pour it back into its cup immediately. You should have a pattern in swirling lines and patches of colour on the inside of your wax shell.

Now repeat the procedure with another colour. Try to make the lines of new colour interact in an interesting way with the first set – and go on in this way until you are satisfied with the coloured pattern inside the shell.

Now you need to fill up the shell with paraffin wax. This is the part of the whole operation that needs the most patience, because it is rather dull, but any undue haste can ruin the shell and its pattern.

Melt the paraffin wax (plain white wax) and keep it at about 190°F. (88°C.). This may seem rather hot for pouring into the delicate shell you have made, but it must be remembered that the wax in the shell is practically cold by the time you have obtained a suitable layer of colour and pattern, but it is necessary to make sure that the wax that fills the shell adheres firmly without any chance of cracks appearing or gaps in the inside of the candle. So some of the heat to make sure that the new wax 'welds' to the shell must come from the wax you are going to pour in now. Pour a tablespoonful of the hot wax into the shell, and rotate the shell as before, making sure that no hot wax is allowed to stay still in any part of the shell. Pour out any wax that seems likely to form a pool, otherwise you will make a hole or dent in the shell. Let the wax set for about twenty seconds and then pour in another table-spoonful, taking the same precautions, and go on like this, very cautiously, until you have built up a layer of wax about ½ in. thick all over the inside of the shell.

When you have got this far, you can speed up the operation, pouring wax in a little at a time. Don't put the shell down on a hard surface until you have built up the ½ in. of wax inside, or it may crush, and make sure it is cold before you treat it any more vigorously than an eggshell. When the shell is nearly full of wax, you can drill a hole for the wick. Lead-stiffened wick is best for this. Select a wick that is smaller than you would need for complete burning, so that the flame forms a deep pool and the light can shine through the wax and show up the coloured patterns (see Table I on page 85 to help you choose the right size of wick). Put the wick into position and top up the cavity with paraffin wax.

When you are pouring the wax into the shell, especially at the critical early stages, quick cooling is a great help to prevent disaster. Some workers use an electric fan to help with this, holding the candle in the stream of air from the fan between putting in spoonfuls of wax.

When you have mastered the technique of making the balloon shells, you will find them a fascinating foundation for the production of all kinds of candles. Instead of simply swirling colour around in the shell, you can, quite simply, draw designs on the inside of the shell so that they show through when the candle is lighted. Use strongly dyed stearin and either a brush or a tjanting. (A tjanting is a kind of brass pen used in batik dyeing work. It has a heavy brass end to hold the heat, and it can be used to draw or write in hot wax.)

If you draw windows on the inside of the shell (see Figure 20) you can make a candle lantern of unusual design. In this case it is better to make the 'top' of the lantern by filling up the last inch of the shell with very dark wax. If you paint a lantern candle like this with traditional Chinese designs you can make a very attractive decoration.

FIG. 20 Lantern balloon. A balloon candle is painted with the lantern 'windows' from inside with a tjanting, and then filled with wax, white wax behind the windows and black wax at the top.

BEESWAX SHEET TECHNIQUES

Beeswax is unique among candle-making waxes because it is extremely flexible, and even thin layers of it can be manipulated with great ease and without much danger of brittleness or cracking (unless the wax is very cold).

For this reason it is possible to make candles from beeswax by rolling up sheets of the wax into the desired shape (this was, in fact, how church candles were made up to quite recently, because beeswax does not easily come out of a mould).

Most candlemakers' suppliers can provide sheets of beeswax, usually about 18 ins. by 9 ins. (or sometimes 17 ins. by $8\frac{1}{2}$ ins) in various colours, and traditionally impressed with a hexagonal pattern like that in a honeycomb. To make candles from this material you need no heating, pouring, moulds, or thermometer, so it is a craft that is particularly useful for children, yet on the other hand, the results can be quite interesting enough to satisfy the most skilled craft worker.

To make a plain cylindrical candle from beeswax sheet, cut a rectangle of the sheet with a sharp knife on a hard surface. A quarter sheet is a good size to start with. Take a length of candlewick about 6 ins. long and lay it along the short side of the sheet, then fasten it to the wax by turning the edge of the sheet over the wick, pressing down gently with the fingers all along the edge so as to fix the wick in a kind of hem of wax. Then, carefully and evenly, roll the wax round until the whole sheet has been formed into a cylinder. Gently press the final edge against the candle to fix it and prevent the cylinder from unrolling. If you do this carefully you can avoid marking the other parts of the candle with your fingers, and depressing the hexagonal markings. This is the main danger in making beeswax sheet candles, but as with any craft, it is easy to pick up the knack of neat working.

If the wax is rather cold, or has been in store for some time, it may not be quite flexible enough for easy rolling. In this case warm it carefully over a heater or in

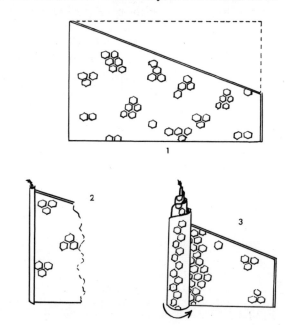

FIG. 21 Beeswax sheet techniques. To make a tapered beeswax candle cut a sheet as shown in (1), fasten the wick at the longest end (2), and roll up the wax sheet (3) into a candle.

warm water (not hot) for a few minutes before starting. Try to avoid the wax sticking to the surface on which you are rolling it. If it sticks it is probably a sign that you are pressing too hard.

To finish off the candle, trim the wick to about $\frac{1}{2}$ in. at the top, and cut it off at the base, and either dip the end of the wick in melted beeswax or press a small piece of beeswax sheet around it with the fingers, so that it is primed with wax ready for lighting.

You can easily make other shapes. If you press the sides of the wax gently against your working surface at intervals as you roll the wax, you can make triangular, square, or hexagonal candles (though don't try to make the corners too sharp, or you may crack the surface of your beeswax sheet).

To make tapered candles, you need to cut the beeswax sheet to form a diagonal edge before rolling (see Figure 21). Lay the sheet on your hard surface, and with a ruler and a sharp knife cut off a triangular piece from the top. The more extreme the angle of your cut, the steeper the taper will be on the finished candle. Lay a wick along the longest side of the cut sheet, and roll up as before, making sure that the base remains level. Finish off the candle as with a cylindrical shape, wax the wick, and check that the base is absolutely flat (if it is not, trim it with a sharp knife).

Most beeswax candles are improved by a small amount of taper, if only to finish off the top to a cone instead of a flat area. If you have beeswax sheets in contrasting colours, you can cut two sheets with parallel sloping tops, and roll them together so that alternate bands of colour spiral down the candle. You will find it convenient to fix the wick into the edge of the largest sheet before you start winding the second sheet into the candle (see Figure 22).

Beeswax sheet can also be cut into thin strips and woven or wound to make surface decorations. For example, make a cylindrical candle out of beeswax sheet, with a very small taper at the top to finish it off. Then cut thin strips, say about $\frac{1}{4}$ in. wide from a sheet in a contrasting colour, and wind these round the candle to form projecting bands, rather like the floors in a pagoda. Or you can wind a thin strip of contrasting beeswax sheet round a rolled candle in the form of a spiral from top to bottom. If you are careful, you can even weave strips of beeswax sheet over the surface of a rolled candle so as to form a complex pattern (see Plate 5).

Make a rolled candle, for example, about 9 ins. high and about 3 ins. in circumference. From another sheet of beeswax in the same colour or a contrasting one, cut off eight strips of wax about $\frac{1}{4}$ in. wide and the same height as the candle. These will form the upright parts of the woven finish. Then cut off twenty-five strips of beeswax again $\frac{1}{4}$ in. wide and about 3 ins. long. These will form the horizontal parts of the weave.

Fix the uprights to the base of the candle by gentle pressure, making sure that they are evenly spaced, and leave them trailing outwards like a bunch of ribbons fastened to the base. Now start to wind the first of your shorter strips round the candle, close to the base, making it go alternately under and over the eight 'uprights'. Carry on like this with the next horizontal strip, reversing the unders and overs, and so on until you have reached the top of the candle. You may not be able to fit in all the twenty-five strips horizontally, or you may need one or two more – it depends how tightly you do your weaving. Finally gently press all the ends into

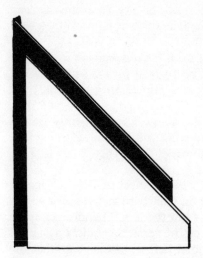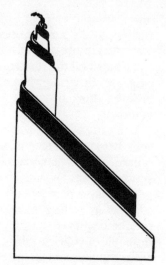

FIG. 22 Beeswax sheet techniques. If you use two sheets of wax in contrasting colours, you can make a striped tapered candle.

the candle to prevent them coming loose, and roll the candle gently on your flat surface to consolidate the weaving.

The odds and ends of beeswax sheet left over from rolling candles can be used in a number of ways. If they are very small they can be added to a paraffin wax blend for moulding or dipping other candles. Beeswax helps to make paraffin wax more opaque, so that colours show up better, and also renders the blend slower burning and rather stronger. Don't add more than one-third of beeswax to blends that you are going to use for moulding, however; otherwise the blend may tend to stick in the mould as beeswax does itself.

If you are doing intaglio work (see p. 38) you will find that beeswax added to soft paraffin wax makes a very useful opaque coating for getting the maximum contrast between the inner and outer colours.

If you have a few larger pieces of beeswax – for example the triangular pieces cut off from the sheet when making tapered candles – try shaping them into little saucers or water-lilies. If you rest a small (not too tall) rolled beeswax candle on these saucers or lilies, you will have a floating candle that can be used in a dish of water or in a garden pool to give light for an outdoor party or barbecue.

Finally, if you get really fascinated by beeswax sheet techniques, you might like to try reviving the early art of wax flower and picture-making in beeswax. This is not strictly candle making, but it may give some ideas for candles of a peculiarly delicate kind.

WAX PICTURES

This art originated in Italy in the seventeenth century and was apparently introduced to England by Mary of Modena, the second wife of James II, in 1686, who brought some very fine examples of wax flowers with her to decorate the rooms of her palace. It became very popular in the nineteenth century, and two brothers

66

called Mintorn ran a 'craft shop' selling supplies for wax flower and picture-making in the Pantheon in Oxford Street, London, and published an instruction book in 1844.

The flowers were made by cutting out each individual leaf and petal from wax, thin sheets of beeswax which had been prepared by pouring the melted wax smoothly over sheets of glass. This not only made even sheets, but provided each sheet of wax with a smooth side, next to the glass, and a slightly rougher side on top, which helped to give a natural look to the petals and leaves cut out of the wax. Mintorns could provide basic colours of white, lemon, yellow, pink, light and dark green, and other tints were produced by painting the petals with tiny quantities of powdered colour as the flowers were built up.

To start a flower, a wire stalk was cut and folded several times near the flower head to make a foundation for the wax. A small piece of appropriately-coloured wax was then rolled round the head of the wire and shaped with the fingers, just like making a rolled beeswax sheet candle. The petals were then cut out of thin wax sheets with scissors, curled with a wire curler to obtain a natural look, and then stuck to the lump of wax forming the head of the flower by pressure. As the brothers Mintorn say, in their instructions for making a *White Camelia* (spelling was obviously different then):

'. . . Half a sheet of White Wax is then rolled around the twisted and compressed wire until it attains the size of a plum-stone. (This is to prevent the possibility of the stem slipping from the flower.) Dip the curling-pin in water. Place the petal flat on the 1st finger of the left hand. The curling pin is to be held in the right so as to rest upon the centre of the upper part of the thumb. To give the actual concavity to each petal, roll the head of the pin close to the edge of the portion of wax in use. Having done this, place the point of the pin in the centre, and consult your taste and judgement till you perceive that you have obtained the required natural form. The first 3 petals are attached close to the plum-stone shaped wax. The 4 following rows, curled similar to the others, are so arranged that each is a little higher than the other so as to avoid one leaf growing absolutely at the back of the other . . .' and so on with the layers of petals, the leaves, and the calyx. The stalk was made by rolling green wax around the wire and attaching the leaves by pressure.

It sounds a long process, but practice soon makes the attachment of the petals almost automatic. A rose candle can be made by similar methods, using beeswax, as follows:

You can use beeswax either in the form of a block of the material, or left-over pieces of wax from making candles in beeswax sheet. Decide on an appropriate colour for your roses. Untreated beeswax, especially unbleached wax, has the ivory to yellow shade of many actual roses, but you may prefer to have a pink or red rose, in which case you must melt the wax and colour it.

Obtain a sheet of glass, window glass or plate glass, or even a glass-topped tray, and polish it with silicone mould release agent. Then warm the tray on a radiator or in front of a heater. Melt the beeswax until it is flowing fairly easily, and pour it over the glass, spreading it if necessary to obtain an even sheet about $\frac{1}{8}$ in. thick. You will probably not be able to make the whole sheet of even thickness, so aim to produce a good deal more wax sheet than you actually need for the petals of your

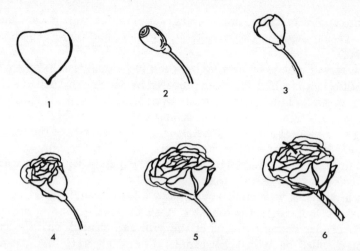

FIG. 23 Rose candle. Cut out rose petals in shape (1) from thin beeswax. Make a stalk of wire and roll a piece of beeswax round it (2), then add on petals, pressing the lower ends of them into the wax ball (3). As you go on, turn some of the petal edges outwards to get the proper rose effect (4) (5). Finally wind green wax round the stalk, add a few green leaves, and fit the wick.

rose, then you can choose the most even bits of the sheet to work with. Let the sheet cool.

Take a length of wire which is stiff enough to stand up by itself and take the weight of the wax rose, and fold over the end three or four times in ¼-in. zig-zags (see Figure 23) finally pushing these together to make a sort of wire knob on the end of the straight portion of the wire. Pick up a portion of your wax (the uneven wax from round the edges of the sheet will do for this part of the work) and roll it round this wire knob, pressing it in with your fingers, and carry on adding wax in this way until you have a shape rather like a small rosebud on the end of the wire.

Now look for the smoothest, thinnest, and most even part of your sheet of rose-coloured wax, lift it carefully with a palette knife, and with a small pair of scissors cut out rose petals, laying each one on the sheet of glass as you finish it. If the scissors stick, dip them into a cup of cold water from time to time.

Pick up each flower petal in turn and carefully fit it to the centre that you have made, pressing the lower part of each petal firmly on to the centre but being careful not to damage or blunt the upper edges of the petals. When you have put on one row of petals, put another row outside these, and turn the edges of these petals slightly outwards. In this way you can build up a flower with a very natural appearance.

Finally drill a hole for the wick very carefully and insert a length of lead-stiffened wick.

You can make the stalk of the rose by winding green beeswax sheet round the wire and pressing it into shape with your fingers. It might be possible to colour the stalk also by dipping it into green wax, but this seems rather risky so near the wax flower.

If you make a bunch of these you can arrange them into a picture, as was done in

68

the nineteenth century, or place them in a vase (alabaster vases were used, and they are now highly prized on the antique market). The only trouble with these decorations as candles is that you will probably not be able to bear to set them alight!

Perhaps one should close this section on the making of wax pictures and flowers by a few words from *The Royal Guide to Wax Flower Modelling* written by Mrs. Emma Peachey in 1856:

'This elegant art requires but the fairy touch of a delicate hand to fill each available space in the chambers or drawing-room with the most perfect and beautiful imitations of the flower garden. Unaffected by change or climate, wax flower modelling perpetuates the transient glories of the floral seasons; places all the tender varieties under the most immediate glance of the ever gratified eye of the artist, who can thus in the depth of winter exhibit to an admiring foreign guest the exotics of a far hemisphere, or the indigenous plants of her own loved land . . .'

Chapter 6

Finishes

There are many things that you can do to a candle to transform its appearance, even after it has come out of the mould or has been dipped for the last time. Some of these methods, like carving back 'chunky' candles, have already been mentioned, but here are some more ideas for getting variety in your candles without having large numbers of moulds or even very elaborate equipment.

HAMMERING

When candle wax is still soft, during its cooling stages, it is very susceptible to pressure, as you will probably have discovered by pressing too hard with your fingers at some critical stage in the production of a candle. If you give a candle in this stage a tap with a hammer or other metal instrument, you will find that the wax bruises easily, and the mark tends to look lighter than the surrounding wax.

A ball-ended hammer, for instance, will leave a circular depression surrounded by a kind of halo of lighter wax, and if you go over the surface of a candle in this way you can build up a pattern of these circular marks that is quite distinctive. A small piece of metal rod or piping can also be used to produce patterns, just by going over the candle with quick sharp blows.

If you are using this technique, remember that the wax changes its characteristics as it cools, so don't spend a long time making an elaborate pattern by hammering on one small area of a candle. You will probably find that you cannot repeat the effect on the rest of the candle because the wax has set and it behaves differently. If you want an all-over design, try to cover the whole area evenly. If you are using a ball-ended hammer, for example, and you intend eventually to cover the whole candle area, work round in circles from bottom to top. Then you know that if the appearance of the dents changes, the candle will still be symmetrical.

Hammering can produce some very pleasant textures on plain candles, and it is often a useful finish to apply if a candle has gone slightly wrong. For example, if you are moulding candles in a metal mould, you may find that some of them are rather disfigured by having a line of little bubbles round them. This is actually caused by not having the cooling water round the mould high enough – it should come right up to the level of the top of the wax – but the problem arises what to do with the candle.

If you want to re-melt it, of course, that is one solution, but alternatively try going over it with a hammer, piece of rod or other heavy tool, or make a pattern of short diagonal lines by working over it quickly with sharp blows from the blunt

70

back of a table knife. The same applies if you have air bubbles on the surface of the candle, due to failure to tap the mould after you poured in the wax. Hammering will hide a multitude of faults.

You will find that it is virtually impossible to make a hammered finish on candles that have been dipped in colour, unless the dipped coating is very thick indeed. Most of the time the effect of hammering is to make the surface coating come away in ugly scales.

APPLIED COLOUR

As well as dipping, you can decorate white candles with colour by sticking pieces of coloured wax on to the surface of the candle. This is another way in which you can use up odds and ends of coloured wax left over from larger candle-making operations.

Melt some strongly coloured wax in a cup or can in your water-bath or a saucepan of water, and pour it on to a sheet of glass or a tray. When it is set, break or carve it into pieces. If you have several colours, treat them in the same way so that you have a collection of small, flat, coloured pieces of wax.

Now make a plain white candle in some fairly simple shape – a square one or a cylinder will be best to start on. When it is complete and cool stand it on a tray or newspaper.

Now you need something to heat a knife blade. Either have boiling water available or use a small spirit lamp. Heat the knife blade (an old table knife will do very well) and hold it against the candle. With your other hand place a piece of the coloured wax on the other side of the knife blade, then slide the knife out and hold the coloured wax in place on the candle until it has 'welded' into place. Go on doing this until you have covered the surface of the white candle with a kaleidoscopic pattern of coloured pieces.

You can use this technique to apply many kinds of decoration to plain candles. Names, initials, symbols, geometrical shapes – anything you can cut out of flat-coloured wax can be applied to a candle.

For example, you can pour out sheets of red wax and black wax, and cut Hearts and Diamonds out of one and Spades and Clubs out of the other. Make a series of square candles, either by moulding or by cutting back with a hot knife from a short fat-dipped candle, in plain white wax, and apply the card symbols to the sides. These will make ideal decorations for a bridge party.

Cut holly leaves out of green wax and the berries out of scarlet wax, and you have the makings of Christmas candles with the minimum of effort or elaboration.

You will soon get the feel of the process, so that your knife is just hot enough to melt a little wax on each surface without spoiling the applied shapes. In these patterned candles, it is usually better to use wicks that are slightly smaller than usual, so that the flames burn down into a hollow and the light shines through the wax to show up the applied decoration.

DRAWING ON CANDLES

You can draw on candles, and often the effects look very fine when the candle is alight and the glow from the wax makes a background to the drawing.

The simplest medium to use is ordinary oil paint or lacquer, which will transfer to the wax surface fairly well. This is often useful for making highlights on a moulded candle with details in relief, as described in Chapter 4, but sometimes you will find that the paint does not 'take' well on the wax surface, and painting with fine detail is rather difficult.

The thing to avoid is getting paint pigment into the well of wax round the wick, otherwise it will block the flow of wax and make the candle burn irregularly.

If you want to get the best results, both in the way of adhesion of your paint to the candle wax, and freedom from interference with the wick, it is best to use coloured wax as your medium. The surface of a candle is very non-absorbent, completely different from paper or textiles, and this is one of the reasons why fluid paints do not always succeed on the surface. If you use coloured wax in the melted state, however, it 'welds' to the surface of the candle, and after it has set it is quite resistant to rubbing and handling. In addition there is the advantage that coloured wax will burn just as easily as the rest of the candle, and cannot interfere with the flow of wax.

The best way of applying your colour to a candle is therefore to dissolve it in stearin or beeswax and 'paint' these waxes on. You can use a brush dipped in the melted coloured wax, or a tjanting (see p. 63). In either case try to work on your design a little at a time so that you can dip your brush or tjanting in the hot coloured wax frequently. This will make sure that your colour flows freely, and save you from getting lumps or dribbles on the candle because of irregular flow of the colour. Simple bold designs look best on candles, for intricate detail tends to get lost to sight when the candle is alight. Chinese characters (see Figure 24) and similar patterns of line are always popular.

FIG. 24 Chinese characters suitable for candles. *Tao* = truth, *Ho* = peace, harmony, *Yin* = secrecy, womanhood, *Yang* = the sun, manhood, *Tê* = virtue, *Chu* = a candle, *Tung* = East and *Hsi* = West.

道	和	陰	陽
Tao	Ho	Yin	Yang

德	燭	東	西
Tê	Chu	Tung	Hsi

Engraving and lining

Some patterns used for decorating candles need very finely drawn, even lines, and these are difficult to do neatly with a brush or tjanting unless you are very skilled at this type of drawing. A method which makes such work easier is a combination of engraving and colouring.

As an example of the method, a *clock candle* is an interesting object to make. Candles for telling the passing of the hours have been in use for many centuries. The scholarly monks writing in their cells by the light of a tallow dip or wax-light must soon have become aware that the candle shortened steadily as the hours passed, and they would soon learn to guess the time to expect nones or matins by a look at the candle. Very soon candles were made with lines drawn on them, marking the hours, and King Alfred the Great, in the ninth century A.D., acquired his unusual amount of learning by reading for a set number of hours each day, regulated by a candle clock. His step-mother Osberga is supposed to have taught him to tell the passing of the hours by the candle as the first stage in his education, otherwise he might have been as illiterate and coarse as the rest of the Saxon kings.

Auctions were often regulated by candle clocks up to quite recent times. In 'candle auctions' in seventeenth-century England an inch of candle was lighted on the autioneers' desk, and bidding could go on until it spluttered out. Sometimes a pin was stuck into the candle a short way down its length: when the pin fell out because the flame had reached it, the last man to bid was awarded the sale. As the

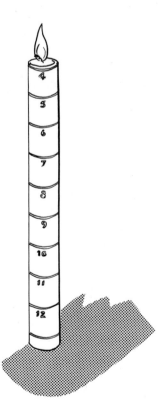

FIG. 25 A clock candle.

auctioneer would have to have a candle to see his papers, this was a very convenient method of keeping the auction lively (in fact, it was traditional at one time for the owners of property to put a note of their 'reserve price', the lowest figure they would accept, under the auctioneer's candlestick, so that it could not be seen by the bidders).

To make such a candle, you first need to know exactly how fast your candle burns. This will obviously vary with the type of wax that you use and the size of the wick, but as a very rough guide, using paraffin wax with 10 per cent of stearin, a 1 in.-diameter candle with the appropriate wick will shorten by about 1 in. per hour, which is a reasonable reduction in size, but still makes it possible to make a twelve-hour candle which is not too tall (Figure 25).

You can either dip the candle or mould it in a convenient container (obviously moulding will give you a more uniform candle). One-inch plastic water piping makes quite a good mould. Make your first candle about 1 in. diameter and just over 1 ft. long, and while you are doing this make another length of candle with the same wax, the same kind of wick, and the same diameter.

When your candles are cool and hardening, take a length of the second candle, cut it off square at top and base, apart from a length of wick at the top, and measure its length carefully. Then set it up out of the draught, light it, and let it burn for exactly 1 hour. Then measure it again. You now know exactly how much your candle will shorten per hour (if you want to be really thorough, repeat the experiment and see whether there is any appreciable difference between the length burned away in the first hour and the second. If there is a difference, take an average).

Suppose you find that with your particular candle and wick $\frac{7}{8}$ in. burns away every hour. You need to mark out your long candle with lines every $\frac{7}{8}$ in. from the top, and number these to show the hours that have passed.

Lay the candle down horizontally on a piece of paper, and mark out the successive $\frac{7}{8}$-in. lines on the paper next to the candle. Now take a small gouge such as is sold for making lino cuts, and carefully cut a 'V'-shaped groove right round the candle opposite each line. Then, with the same gouge, carve the numbers 1, 2, 3, and so on down the candle. These grooves and numbers should be about $\frac{1}{8}$ in. deep, not more and not much less. You will find that a lino-cutting tool carves the wax very easily and smoothly.

Now make up a strong solution of colour – red or black looks well for these candles – in beeswax. Put the coloured hot wax in a small tjanting and carefully go over the grooves, filling them with coloured wax. Try to be as neat as you can, but don't worry if your lines do not exactly fit the grooves, as long as the grooves are filled: if necessary go over again with the tjanting. If the tjanting gets cold and the wax stops flowing, heat it up again. If it gets clogged, heat it gently and blow through it, or if necessary poke the blockage out with a piece of very fine wire.

Now leave the candle to cool – which will not take long because there is not very much hot beeswax on it – and go over the design carefully with the edge of a sharp craft knife or a chisel edge, removing all the coloured wax that is above the surface of the grooves, and any colour that has strayed off the proper line. You should be left with grooves accurately filled with colour, looking as if they have been engraved into the wax – which, in fact, they have.

74

This technique can obviously be used for any other designs that need unusually accurate work and clean lines. It was used extensively in the nineteenth century for decorating candles.

Chapter 7

Some Special Effects

The first 'special effect' worth mentioning is in fact the simplest way of making candles that there is – just pour coloured wax into containers, fit a wick, and there is your candle.

For example, if you crack walnuts carefully so that you have the two halves of the shell intact, you can pour coloured wax into these little bowls, let it set, and then drill a hole for a small length of wick of appropriate size. These candles will make small 'boats' that can be floated on a pond or in a large bowl of water for an outdoor party or barbecue. They will burn for about an hour with luck, before the wick tips over and extinguishes itself. You could obviously do the same with larger nutshells, such as coconut shells, and make long-lasting candles.

Many people make candles in glasses or jars of attractive shape. These do not have to be very expensive or exceptional containers, as you can brighten them up by using the various multicoloured wax techniques described in Chapter 4. Striped candles look very good in a thin glass – pour the wax at about 180°F. (82°C.) and let each layer get to the 'rubbery' stage before you pour on the next one. Or you can cut coloured chunks and pack them round the sides of the glass, and then cover them with white or light-coloured wax as background. In either case, it is best to drill a hole for the wick after you have completed the candle, and use lead-stiffened wick to push down into the hole (alternatively you can make a free-standing lead-stiffened wick, as described on page 22, and balance this in the glass before you start pouring the wax. However, some glasses are so curved at the bottom that it is difficult to get the wick to stand up properly until you have at least one layer of wax in place).

If you have some brownish wax left over from a mixture of colours – for example when a multicoloured candle has gone wrong and you have had to re-melt all the colours together – you can shade this to the same sort of brown as beer, and pour it into an appropriate-shaped beer glass to set. Leave a little room on top and put a layer of froth on it, using white whipped wax, then fit the whole thing with a wick.

TRANSPARENT CANDLES
There have been recipes for making candle wax mixtures that are transparent, or nearly so, but most of them are too soft to make a very successful candle of the conventional type. However, if you make your candles in a glass you can use wax blends that are very much softer than usual, as long as the wick is held firmly.

If you want to make a candle in a glass that looks like a glass of red wine, for instance, make a red candle by dipping a wick of the right size and length for your glass into ordinary paraffin wax/stearin blend that has been coloured deep red. Carry on dipping until you have a candle that is about ½ in. in diameter. It helps if you dip a little more at the base of the candle than at the top, so that it is rather conical. This ensures that it will stand up safely in the glass.

Stick it to the glass, in the middle, by melting a little of the wax on the base of the candle and pressing it down. You can either warm the base of the candle with a hot knife or warm the glass where you want the candle to stick depending on the shape of the glass and whether the stem is in the way.

Now, while the red candle is cooling, make up the following wax blend:

Paraffin wax – hard (melting-point 130–135°F.), 70 per cent

Stearin, 15 per cent

Liquid paraffin (mineral oil), 15 per cent.

This last ingredient is the common medicinal mineral oil. It adds to the transparency of the mixture, but obviously also softens it. Dye this mixture to a wine colour, using colour dissolved in stearin, and pour it round the candle already in the glass. If you have a good grade of mineral oil it should look very effective. The inner candle is to provide a core of harder wax that will hold up the wick safely, even when the heat of the flame has softened the surrounding blend of wax and oil.

COLOURED FLAMES

You must have noticed that if you throw salt on an open fire, the flames burn yellow, and sometimes if you burn packaging material bright green and blue flames come up. This is because all metals give a characteristic colour to flames (in the case of the packaging materials, it is usually compounds of copper in the printing inks that give the green or blue flames).

This characteristic is used by scientists to detect the various metals, the colours being determined by an instrument called a spectroscope, and it is used by firework manufacturers to produce coloured flames and sparks from their products. Almost any compounds of the metals can be used, but usually compounds are selected that will also help with the proper combustion of the firework.

The following colours can be obtained in flames quite brightly:

Sodium compounds give a *yellow* flame (very bright, it tends to mask other colours).

Potassium compounds give a *lilac* flame.

Lithium compounds give a *red* flame.

Calcium compounds give a *brick red* flame (not very bright).

Strontium compounds give a *crimson* flame.

Barium compounds give a *bright green* flame.

These last two are very bright, and are used extensively in the manufacture of fireworks and coloured flares.

Copper compounds give a *greenish-blue* flame.

Some *boron* compounds give a *green-edged* flame.

Compounds of these metals can be used to give their characteristic colours to candle flames by soaking the wick in a solution of the compound, and then letting it dry. If you are careful, you can soak different portions of the wick in different salts and get a change of colour as the candle burns down, and some suppliers sell wicks prepared in this way. There are, however, one or two disadvantages.

Firstly, some of these compounds are dangerous. All *barium* compounds, for example, are POISONOUS, and should not be handled except with great care. This is rather a pity, because barium gives undoubtedly the brightest green colour to a flame. Copper compounds are also poisonous, although not to the same degree as barium.

The second objection is more serious in its way. Candle flames are characteristically bright yellow, and in practice this yellow colour tends to mask any very bright colours induced by the metals added to the wick. The coloured flames are not at all in the same class as coloured firework flames. What is really needed is a wax blend for making the candles that produces a hotter and less yellow flame, so that the colours produced by the metals and their compounds can be seen clearly. Mixtures are available for improving the candle blends in this way, but they are not really suitable for mixing up at home without a reasonable amount of chemical apparatus and experience. They are, however, obtainable from a few suppliers.

Chapter 8

Faults

Odd and unexpected things happen to every candlemaker at times, and occasionally a candle turns out with serious faults. This is not a disaster in itself, but it is always better to know what went wrong so that you can avoid it happening again.

This chapter may sound depressing if you read it straight through, as if no candle had any reasonable chance of coming out right. In fact, most candles turn out right even the first time you do them and this chapter is just something to turn to on the odd occasions when they don't. Each fault is given in turn, with the likely cause and the best remedy, if there is a remedy apart from re-melting and starting again.

Faults in dipped candles
1. *Candle has a lumpy surface or little spots like pimples.*
    CAUSE: Candle has been dipped too cold at some point in the process. Probably the wax was allowed to cool too much.
    REMEDY: Melt some wax the same colour as the outside layer of the candle, heat to 200°F. (93°C.) and re-dip candle until outside layer is smooth.

2. *Candle cracks while it is being rolled or twisted.*
    CAUSE: Candle has been allowed to cool too much before rolling or twisting, or possibly has been allowed to hang up too long between layers, so that the inside is colder than the outside.
    REMEDY: If the crack is very bad (i.e. the wax actually flaking away) re-melt and start again. If the cracks are just internal ones and the candle is still complete, re-dip in hot wax the same colour as the outside layer, at about 200°F. (93°C.), until the candle is pliable. If you can only *hear* it beginning to crack you can often save it by immersing it in water at about 130°F. (54°C.) and keeping it there until it becomes pliable.

3. *White marks between the layers of cut-back multilayered candles.*
    CAUSE: The candle has been left too long between dips of colour.
    REMEDY: If you have only just started cutting out the shapes in the surface of the candle, dip it in wax the same colour as the outside layer at 200°F. (93°C.) until it feels more pliable. You will have to cut away the layer of extra wax over the hole that you have made. If you have already cut out the shapes you want and you cannot afford to have a layer of coloured wax over them, dip the candle in water at about 150°F. (66°C.) and leave it there for about twenty minutes to soften through. This does not always work.

4. *Coloured layer flakes off during rolling.*

CAUSE: Candle too cold or layer of colour too thin.

REMEDY: In either case dip the candle in the outside coloured wax at 200°F. (93°C.) until it is more pliable. If the outside flakes off during *hammering* this type of candle, this, I am afraid, is usual.

5. *Pear-shaped and other 'shaped' candles not symmetrical.*

CAUSE: Candle has not been rotated enough during dipping. Often, even with the best heating set-up, the temperature of the dipping wax varies from one part to another of the melting pot, and this shows if you are dipping a fat candle.

REMEDY: Shave off the bulges with a sharp knife, mould the candle to approximately the right shape between your hands, and re-dip to smooth it out.

6. *Candle flame spits when burning.*

CAUSE: Water has got into the wick during dipping.

REMEDY: Sometimes you can get rid of the water by pouring out the melted wax from the well under the wick and the water may go with it. If this does not work, re-melt and start again. Always try to make sure that wicks are thoroughly waxed before you dip candles in water.

7. *Scum or dirty marks form on the candle while it is being dipped.*

CAUSE: Impurities in the water, corrosion of the melting vessel, or dirty wax remelted. (You may have re-melted an unsuccessful candle and got some black bits from the wick mixed up with the wax.)

REMEDY: Ladle off scum from the surface of the melted wax and raise the temperature to about 200°F. (93°C.). Then re-dip to clean up the candle surface.

Faults in moulded candles

8. *Wax leaks out of base of mould during pouring.*

CAUSE: Wick has come unfixed or the hole for the wick is too large.

REMEDY: Use mould seal or modelling clay to fill the gap. Quite often, when you fit a well-waxed wick into a mould, it seems securely fixed just because of the wax on it. When you pour in hot wax, however, the wax on the wick melts and it comes loose in the hole. This is a particular problem with metal and other rigid moulds – rubber moulds tend to grip the wick better.

9. *Pits in surface of candle.*

CAUSE: Air bubbles in the mould, or moisture left in the mould after washing.

REMEDY: There is no way to remedy this fault except by covering the surface over with paint, or hammering, and similar processes. Always tap the mould several times to release air just after the wax has been poured, and always make sure that the mould is clean and dry before you use it.

10. *Scaly marks on the surface of the candle.*

CAUSE: The wax was poured too cold, or the mould was very cold, and wax has set on the inside of the mould before pouring was completed.

REMEDY: A dip in hot wax of the same colour at 200°F. (93°C.) will sometimes cure this fault, but often the only solution is to re-melt and start again. Make sure that the wax is hotter than 170°F. (77°C.) before pouring, except for special processes like using whipped wax. These scales can also occur if a metal mould is used immersed in the cooling water before the wax is poured. Again the wax sets on the surface of the mould in irregular shapes before pouring is complete, and these show up as marks on the surface of the finished candle.

11. *Misshapen candle.*
CAUSE: With rubber moulds, the usual cause is that the mould has sagged on its support. Sometimes this happens when a mould is getting rather old and thin, or if you habitually pour your wax too hot – it should not be over 180°F. (82°C.) for rubber moulds. With metal and other rigid moulds, the usual cause of bad shape is that the wax has not been topped up regularly during the cooling stage, and shrinkage has been irregular.
REMEDY: If the candle is in a rubber mould and still warm, it can often be pressed back into shape carefully between the hands. With metal moulds, or if the candle is cold and has been turned out of the mould before you notice the faulty shape, the only remedy is to remelt.

12. *Large cracks in the candle.*
CAUSE: These are thermal cracks, caused by cooling the candle too rapidly.
REMEDY: There is no remedy for these cracks. Re-melt the candle, or cut it up to make chunks for other candles. You should avoid cooling that is too rapid – putting the candle in a refrigerator, for example. In winter, make sure that your candle is not in an icy draught as it cools.

13. *Candle sticks in the mould.*
CAUSE: The wax blend may be wrong – stearin or beeswax should always be present to make sure that the mixture contracts as it cools in the mould. The topping-up process may have introduced a wedge of wax at the top of the candle which makes it difficult to get out of the mould.
REMEDY: Place the mould in hot water at about 200°F. (93°C.) briefly to melt the surface of the wax. Don't leave it in the water long, or you may spoil the surface gloss of the candle. Make sure that the trouble is not due merely to the wick sticking in its hole – you can melt this out with a hot knife applied to the mould where the wick goes through.

14. *Small bubbly line around the candle.*
CAUSE: The cooling water round the mould did not reach up to the same level as the wax. The bubbled line represents the height of the water: the wax above this line cooled much slower than the wax below, so there is a stress mark.
REMEDY: This fault can sometimes be cured by dipping the candle in hot wax of the same colour at about 200°F. (93°C.) but usually it is necessary to cover up the fault by painting or hammering the candle. Always try to adjust the water in your cooling bath or bucket so that the water level is the same as the level of wax in the filled mould.

15. *Gaps in whipped wax candles.*

CAUSE: The wax has not been pushed down firmly enough, and air spaces have been left in the mould. Always tap the mould down as you fill, to shake down the whipped wax, or press the wax in firmly with your fingers.

REMEDY: A dip in hot wax may help to improve the look of the candle, if the gaps are not too large. Otherwise re-melt and start again.

16. *'Ice candles' will not burn properly.*

CAUSE: The wick was not sufficiently well waxed before the ice was put in the mould, and water has soaked into it as the ice melted. The wick for ice candles should always be covered with a thick layer of wax by dipping before it is fitted into the mould.

REMEDY: Sometimes the water will dry out of the candle by itself, if the candle is left standing in a warm place for a few days. Otherwise pour off the molten wax from the pool round the wick when spluttering starts, and relight the candle.

Faults with multicoloured candles

17. *Background colour of chunky candles becomes discoloured.*

CAUSE: The background wax was too hot when poured, and it has melted the chunks and mixed with them. Wax for chunky candles should be poured at 200°F (93°C.).

REMEDY: Carve away the background wax with a sharp knife. You can either eave the candle this way, as a carved shape, or go on to dissect it still further, cut out the chunks, and start again.

18. *Layers in multilayered candles have not joined.*

CAUSE: The wax was poured at too low a temperature, or the layers had been allowed to set too much before the next lot of wax was poured. For making layered candles the wax should always be poured at about 180°F. (82°C.) and left until the surface is just 'rubbery' before the next lot of wax is poured on top. It is better to melt all your colours together and keep them at the right temperature, rather than melting them one after another, because if you have them all ready you can concentrate on pouring at just the right moment.

REMEDY: There is no remedy for cracking or badly joined multicoloured candles. Re-melt and use the mixed coloured wax that you will obtain (it is usually brown or grey) for 'antique' effects. Alternatively you can cut carefully along each join and use the pieces of coloured wax for chunks, or to stick on the surface of white candles by welding with a hot knife (see page 71).

19. *Edges of layers not straight in multicoloured candles.*

CAUSE: The lower layer has been allowed to set too much before the next colour was poured on top. This means that the lower layer has had the opportunity to shrink away from the mould, and wax from the next layer has run down into the gaps at the side. Always pour when the lower layer is just rubbery.

REMEDY: Shave around the sides of the candle with a sharp knife to remove the unwanted streaks of colour. A very quick dip in hot plain white wax (at about 210°F.,

99°C.) or boiling water may help to clean up the lines after you have shaved off the worst of the streaks.

20. *Layers have run together in multicoloured candles.*
CAUSE: The wax has been poured too hot or too soon, so that the coloured waxes have mixed along the edges of the layers.
REMEDY: There is no remedy for this. If the effects of the mixed colours are at all pleasing, you might try putting the candle back in its mould and exaggerating the mixing effect by immersing the mould in hot water. If this is not an effective solution to the problem, remelt and use the mixed wax for antique effects.

Faults with shell or balloon candles
21. *The shell of a balloon candle cracks during colouring.*
CAUSE: Usually caused by the use of wax with too high a melting-point, or ordinary candle wax blends. The addition of stearin to most candles is a necessity, but stearin and other high-melting-point waxes in balloon candles tend to spoil the translucency of the wax, and often also cause cracks.
REMEDY: There is no remedy for a cracked balloon candle. Re-melt the wax for use in coloured blends.

22. *The shell of a balloon candle sags out of shape.*
CAUSE: The wax has not cooled enough before the balloon was removed from the inside, or hot wax has been allowed to remain in one spot during the filling stage.
REMEDY: There is no remedy. Re-melt the wax and, if it has not been coloured, it can be used for making another balloon candle, or otherwise blended into ordinary candle wax with stearin or beeswax.

Faults with wicks
23. *Wax runs down the candle in streams, and the well round the wick becomes flooded and overflows.*
CAUSE: Wick too large for the diameter of the candle or the type of wax used. Waxes (like paraffin wax) which melt very easily need a smaller wick than beeswax or stearin.

24. *Candle smokes badly, and the flame is very large.*
CAUSE: Wick is too large for the diameter of the candle or the type of wax used.

25. *Candle burns very poorly, and easily goes out.*
CAUSE: Usually the cause of this fault is that the wick is too small for the diameter of the candle or the type of wax. Paraffin wax can easily flood a small wick if the diameter of the wick pool is large, while waxes like beeswax and stearin need a larger, looser wick than ordinary paraffin wax blends.
REMEDY: There are really no *remedies* for these faults, except choosing a more appropriate wick for the next candle you make.

Appendix

TABLE I: HOW TO SELECT WICKS FOR YOUR CANDLES
(The numbers refer to standard wicks made of three bundles of strands plaited together. For example, 3/14 means three bundles of 14 strands each plaited together.)

Average diameter of candle	WICKS TO SELECT FOR			
	Paraffin Wax (normal burning)	Beeswax (normal burning)	Paraffin Wax (hollow)	Beeswax (hollow)
½ in.	3/6	3/10	3/4	3/6
1 in.	3/10	3/20	3/6	3/14
1½ in.	3/14	3/24	3/10	3/20
2 in.	3/20	3/30	3/14	3/24
2½ in.	3/24	3/35	3/20	3/30
3 in.	3/30	3/40	3/24	3/35
4 in.	3/35	—	3/30	3/40
More than 4 ins.	3/40	—	3/35	3/40

'Hollow' burning is allowing a large candle to burn with a small wick so that a hollow is formed as the wax is consumed, and finally the glow of the flame is seen through a shell of wax. It is not usually possible to make a candle burn in this way to produce a hollow deeper than about 5–5½ ins.

TABLE II: HOW MUCH WAX YOU WILL NEED FOR VARIOUS MOULDS

CYLINDRICAL MOULDS

	WEIGHTS OF WAX IN OZS.					
Height in ins.	Average diameter in ins.					
	1	$1\frac{1}{2}$	2	$2\frac{1}{2}$	3	4
1	$\frac{1}{2}$	1	$1\frac{3}{4}$	$2\frac{3}{4}$	$3\frac{3}{4}$	$6\frac{3}{4}$
$1\frac{1}{2}$	$\frac{3}{4}$	$1\frac{1}{2}$	$2\frac{1}{2}$	4	$4\frac{3}{4}$	10
2	1	2	$3\frac{1}{4}$	$5\frac{1}{4}$	$7\frac{1}{2}$	$13\frac{1}{4}$
$2\frac{1}{2}$	$1\frac{1}{4}$	$2\frac{1}{2}$	$3\frac{1}{4}$	$6\frac{1}{2}$	$9\frac{1}{4}$	$16\frac{1}{2}$
3	$1\frac{1}{4}$	3	5	$7\frac{3}{4}$	$11\frac{1}{4}$	$19\frac{3}{4}$
4	$1\frac{3}{4}$	$3\frac{3}{4}$	$6\frac{1}{4}$	$10\frac{1}{4}$	$14\frac{3}{4}$	$26\frac{1}{4}$
5	$2\frac{1}{4}$	$4\frac{3}{4}$	$8\frac{1}{4}$	13	$18\frac{1}{2}$	$32\frac{1}{4}$
6	$2\frac{1}{2}$	$5\frac{3}{4}$	10	$15\frac{1}{2}$	$22\frac{1}{4}$	$39\frac{1}{2}$
7	3	$6\frac{1}{2}$	$11\frac{1}{2}$	18	26	46
8	$3\frac{1}{2}$	$7\frac{1}{2}$	$13\frac{1}{4}$	$20\frac{1}{2}$	$29\frac{1}{2}$	$52\frac{1}{4}$
9	$3\frac{3}{4}$	$8\frac{1}{2}$	$14\frac{3}{4}$	$23\frac{1}{4}$	$33\frac{1}{4}$	59
10	$4\frac{1}{4}$	$9\frac{1}{4}$	$16\frac{1}{2}$	$25\frac{3}{4}$	37	$65\frac{1}{2}$
11	$4\frac{1}{2}$	$10\frac{1}{4}$	18	$28\frac{1}{4}$	$40\frac{1}{2}$	72
12	5	$11\frac{1}{4}$	$19\frac{3}{4}$	$30\frac{3}{4}$	$44\frac{1}{4}$	$78\frac{3}{4}$

CYLINDRICAL MOULDS

	WEIGHTS OF WAX IN GRAMS					
Height in centimetres	Average diameter in centimetres					
	2	3	4	5	7	10
2	6	13	23	34	70	142
5	15	32	57	89	173	354
10	29	64	113	177	346	707
15	43	96	170	265	519	1060
20	57	127	226	353	693	1413
25	71	159	282	442	865	1767
30	85	191	339	530	1038	2120

CONICAL MOULDS

Height of cone in ins.	WEIGHTS OF WAX IN OUNCES					
	Average diameter of base in ins.					
	1	$1\frac{1}{2}$	2	$2\frac{1}{2}$	3	4
1	$\frac{1}{4}$	$\frac{1}{2}$	$\frac{3}{4}$	1	$1\frac{1}{4}$	$2\frac{1}{4}$
2	$\frac{1}{2}$	$\frac{3}{4}$	1	$1\frac{3}{4}$	$2\frac{1}{2}$	$4\frac{1}{2}$
3	$\frac{1}{2}$	1	$1\frac{3}{4}$	$2\frac{1}{4}$	$3\frac{3}{4}$	$6\frac{3}{4}$
4	$\frac{3}{4}$	$1\frac{1}{4}$	$2\frac{1}{4}$	$3\frac{1}{2}$	5	$8\frac{3}{4}$
5	$\frac{3}{4}$	$1\frac{3}{4}$	$2\frac{3}{4}$	$4\frac{1}{2}$	$6\frac{1}{4}$	11
6	1	2	$3\frac{1}{2}$	$5\frac{1}{4}$	$7\frac{1}{2}$	$13\frac{1}{4}$
7	1	$2\frac{1}{4}$	4	6	$8\frac{3}{4}$	$15\frac{1}{2}$
8	$1\frac{1}{4}$	$2\frac{1}{2}$	5	7	10	$17\frac{1}{2}$
9	$1\frac{1}{4}$	3	5	$7\frac{1}{4}$	$11\frac{1}{4}$	$19\frac{3}{4}$
10	$1\frac{1}{2}$	$3\frac{1}{4}$	$5\frac{1}{2}$	$8\frac{3}{4}$	$12\frac{1}{2}$	22
11	$1\frac{1}{2}$	$3\frac{1}{2}$	6	$9\frac{1}{2}$	$13\frac{1}{2}$	24
12	$1\frac{3}{4}$	$3\frac{3}{4}$	$6\frac{3}{4}$	$10\frac{1}{4}$	$14\frac{1}{2}$	$26\frac{1}{4}$

CONICAL MOULDS

Height of cone in cms.	WEIGHTS OF WAX IN GRAMS					
	Average diameter of base in cms.					
	2	3	4	5	7	10
2	2	5	8	12	24	48
5	5	11	19	30	58	118
10	10	22	38	59	116	236
15	15	32	57	89	173	354
20	19	43	76	118	231	471
25	24	53	94	148	289	589
30	29	64	113	177	346	707

TABLE III: FAHRENHEIT AND CENTIGRADE (CELSIUS) THERMOMETER SCALES

°F.	°C.	°F.	°C.	°F.	°C.	°F.	°C.	°F.	°C.
32	0	115	46	200	93	284	140	365	185
35	2	120	49	203	95	285	141	370	188
40	4	122	50	205	96	290	143	374	190
41	5	125	52	210	99	293	145	375	191
45	7	130	54	212	100	295	146	380	193
50	10	131	55	215	102	300	149	383	195
55	13	135	57	220	104	302	150	385	196
59	15	140	60	221	105	305	152	390	199
60	16	145	63	225	107	310	154	392	200
65	18	149	65	230	110	311	155	395	202
68	20	150	66	235	113	315	157	400	204
70	21	155	68	239	115	320	160	401	205
75	24	158	70	240	116	325	163		
77	25	160	71	245	118	329	165		
80	27	165	74	248	120	330	166		
85	29	167	75	250	121	335	168		
86	30	170	77	255	124	338	170		
90	32	175	79	257	125	340	171		
95	35	176	80	260	127	345	174		
100	38	180	82	265	129	347	175		
104	40	185	85	266	130	350	177		
105	41	190	88	270	132	355	179		
110	43	194	90	275	135	356	180		
113	45	195	91	280	138	360	182		

TABLE IV: MELTING POINTS OF SOME CANDLE-MAKING WAXES

Wax	°F.	°C.
Candlenut wax	68–70	20–21
Bayberry wax	75–77	24–25
Coconut oil	75–81	24–27
Palm kernel oil	77–82	25–28
Spermaceti	106–120	41–49
Beef tallow	108–111	42–44
Very soft paraffin wax	110–112	43–44
Myrtle wax	116–118	47–48
Soft paraffin wax grade 1	118–120	48–49
Cocoa butter	118–127	48–53
Soft paraffin wax grade 2	125–130	52–54
Hard paraffin wax grade 1	130–135	54–57
Soft microcrystalline wax	130–140	54–60
Hard paraffin wax grade 2	135–140	57–60
Beeswax	144–151	62–66
Stearin	153–157	67–69
Ozokerite (ceresin)	167–171	75–77
Hard microcrystalline wax	175–180	79–88
Montan wax	176–187	80–86
Carnauba wax	186–192	86–89

TABLE V: CANDLE (EQUIPMENT) SUPPLIERS

A. Sgritta Co.	94 Spencer Street Brooklyn, N.Y.
Beacon Chemical Corp.	244 Lafayette Street New York, N.Y.
Berje Chemical Products Corp.	43–10 23rd Street Long Island City, New York
Devoe Night Light Accessory Co.	289 North 7th Street Brooklyn, New York
Skaron Narrow Fabric Inc.	99 W. Hawthorne Ave Valley Stream, Long Island, New York

Index